Refresh Your Life
in the Spirit

Refresh Your Life in the Spirit

BABSIE BLEASDELL
WITH HENRY LIBERSAT

SERVANT PUBLICATIONS
ANN ARBOR, MICHIGAN

Charis Books is an imprint of Servant Publications especially designed to serve Roman Catholics.

Scripture texts used in this work are taken from the *New American Bible with Revised New Testament,* © 1986, 1970 Confraternity of Christian Doctrine, Washington, D.C. and are used by permission of the copyright owner. All rights reserved. No part of the *New American Bible* may be reproduced in any form without permission in writing from the copyright owner.

Published by Servant Publications
P.O. Box 8617
Ann Arbor, Michigan 48107

Cover design: Hile Illustration and Design, Ann Arbor, Michigan
Cover photo: © Bill Ross/Westlight

98 99 00   10 9 8 7 6 5 4 3 2

Printed in the United States of America
ISBN 1-56955-022-0

Library of Congress Cataloging-in-Publication Data

Bleasdell, Babsie.
Refresh your life in the spirit / Babsie Bleasdell, with Henry Libersat.
    p.   cm. — (Celebrate 2000! series)
ISBN 1-56955-022-0 (alk. paper)
1. Spiritual life—Catholic Church.   2. Holy Spirit.   I. Libersat, Henry.   II. Title.   III. Series.
BX2350.2.B54   1997
231'.3—dc21   97-22779
                                          CIP

Dedication

This book is dedicated to the Immaculate Heart of Mary, who is my hope and inspiration. It is also dedicated to my two natural daughters, Erica and Paula, and their families, who have so often been deprived of my maternal presence as I ran around the world for the sake of the gospel.

And, I also dedicate this work to my many children in the Spirit. God bless you all!

Contents

Acknowledgments

Many, many friends, both priests and laity, have encouraged me to write what I believe and have experienced. They have repeatedly insisted that I had something to say and had the ability to do so. They are too numerous to mention, but to all of them I say, "Thank you!"

A special "thank you" to Father Michael Moses for his dedication in reading the manuscript critically and to Father Ian Taylor who came and read to me when my eyes failed as I tried to review the draft. He also provided typing help through friends. How does one thank friends for such tender, loving care?

My gratitude also goes to Peggy Libersat who hosted me in her home for one whole week as her husband, Deacon Henry, and I plugged away at the interviews that preceded the writing of this book. Peggy patiently tended to all my needs and shared her family ungrudgingly. And, of course, I thank Henry as my coauthor in this effort.

Finally, but not least, I am grateful to the members of the Word of Life Prayer Community who picked up all the slack while I hibernated to produce this book!

Babsie Bleasdell

Introduction

~~~~

Just who is the Holy Spirit? How can we know him, recognize his presence? What is his role in our lives? What does he do for us as we strive to live the gospel of the Lord?

There are tried and true answers to these questions, but for most of us the answers have been all too heady, with too little heart. It is one thing to *say* that God is one God, and that there are three Persons in that one God (each Person fully and completely God). It is quite another to be able to embrace that mystery with joyful trust, with an understanding spirit born of faith. Reciting doctrinal truths does not faith make. Even Satan knows there are three Persons in one God.

What God wants of us is to know him, to love him and to serve him in this life and to be happy with him in the next. That's the answer from the old *Baltimore Catechism,* but it's a good answer to this day. It's the kind of answer that should excite the human heart, which yearns for God because it is made in the image of God. It is made to be with God. That is why St. Augustine said, "Our hearts are restless until they rest in you."

God is Father, Creator, Forgiver. God is Son, Savior, Redeemer, Leader. God is Holy Spirit, Comforter, Paraclete, Advocate, Healer.

This book is about the third Person of God, the Holy Spirit. It challenges us to see the Holy Spirit as the Life Giver, who makes grace happen in everyday situations. It is the Holy Spirit, the very love of God, who makes sacraments become realities. It is the Holy Spirit's power that changes bread and wine into the Body and Blood of Jesus Christ. It is the Holy Spirit who makes a man and woman one in flesh and spirit in holy matrimony. And it is the same Spirit that gives a man the power to be priest for the people of God, to make Eucharist happen at Mass, to forgive sins in the name of our Triune God.

Anyone who wants to see how the Holy Spirit works needs only to look at the saints, whose lives of heroic virtue demonstrate the Spirit's presence and action. Sir Thomas More was beheaded by Henry VIII when he steadfastly refused to acknowledge the king's adulterous second marriage and his claim to be head of the Church. Not martyrdom, however, but the faith that comes from the Holy Spirit makes saints. This faith gave Sir Thomas More, Lord Chancellor of England, the strength to give heroic witness to the Catholic faith through his life ... and in death.

Consider, too, St. Henry, a German king and emperor who never shed his blood for the faith but who used his prestige, power, and wealth to expand the kingdom of God. And there is our beloved St. Francis of Assisi, who by choosing poverty was blessed by the wealth of the Holy Spirit and became a force of renewal within the Church.

Elizabeth Ann Seton was a wife, widow, and ultimately a nun. She became a saint not by running away from the world, but by letting the Holy Spirit teach her how to embrace her responsibilities and reach out to children other than her own. This poor, lonely woman became the mother of both the public and parochial school systems in the United States.

St. Augustine, as we know, was quite a carouser, a scoundrel in many ways, until his restless heart at last found rest in God. His writings and teachings, inspired by the Holy Spirit, have been both light and inspiration for generations of Christians.

Mary, the Mother of Jesus, our saint of all saints, Queen of Apostles and Angels, chose God's will above her own. It is in her "fiat," her acceptance of God's will, that we discover truly the power and role of the Holy Spirit. When she said "yes" to God, she became pregnant with Jesus through the power of the Holy Spirit. When we say "yes" to God, we too in a sense become "pregnant" with Jesus.

At baptism, we are "overshadowed" by the same Holy Spirit who overshadowed Mary. She conceived Jesus in her womb. We "conceive" him in our hearts. *We* become Christ bearers who bring him into the world through our very lives of faith and commitment. Through the power of the Holy Spirit, we bring Jesus into the home and school, into the marketplace and industry, into friendships and strained relationships, into politics and governments, into medicine and other sciences.

When you stop to think about it, this is what millions of people do every day, in cooperation with the Holy Spirit. They say "yes" to God as they embrace the sometimes heartbreaking tasks of rearing their children, paying their bills, caring for aging parents, comforting their neighbors and contributing to the common good by promoting peace, justice, and harmony in communities. They say "yes" to God as they sit in lonely old age, so often neglected by their loved ones, but loving them and praying for them anyway. Young people say "yes" to God when they strive to live chaste lives against overwhelming odds, resisting the pressure of peer groups and gangs, reaching out in love to build houses with Habitat for Humanity or to assist the poor of Appalachia.

We all face challenges in life—from tasks too difficult to accomplish to temptations seemingly too powerful to resist. Yet we often accomplish the impossible and succeed, at least sometimes, in resisting those powerful temptations. None of this is possible without the Holy Spirit.

In this book, *Refresh Your Life in the Spirit,* you will meet

Auntie Babsie, a charming woman who is known throughout the world as a lay evangelist and convincing witness to the power of the Holy Spirit's action in the life of believers. She will share her walk with God, and her particular experience of the Holy Spirit in and through the charismatic renewal. She will express her unshakable faith that all Christians can benefit from the gifts of the Holy Spirit in a way that will enable them to be themselves—and yet to be open to the call and power of God.

Babsie Bleasdell, born in 1921 into a Catholic family in Trinidad, has discovered what she calls the ultimate joy—to be one with Jesus Christ, through the power of the Holy Spirit. Her journey—from a life lived in unconscious grace to a life of constant awareness of God's presence and power—has not been easy. But Auntie Babsie made that journey, and she tells us in this book how she did it, and how we can do it as well.

For more than five decades, this remarkable woman has gradually grown in wisdom. She has experienced an intimate relationship with God through the power of the Holy Spirit. She discovered just how much God wanted to be a part of her life. She surrendered to God and she became victorious over fear, anxiety and the people who would have harmed her. She has shared her story in her own native Trinidad, throughout the United States and Canada, in Holland and South America. She has even spoken to an audience of five thousand Catholic priests in St. Peter's Basilica in Rome.

In this book Auntie Babsie calls readers to the possibilities of a faith they may never have dreamed possible—a faith that truly sets captives free, opens the eyes of the spiritually blind, heals broken bodies and hearts, and brings health and wholeness to family and community relationships.

This book is not for the idly curious, although the idly curious may indeed find something for which they have long and perhaps unconsciously been looking.

And this book is not for people looking for deep theological arguments, although Auntie Babsie's Catholic spirituality is rooted in sound and traditional theology.

Rather, *Refresh Your Life in the Spirit* is written for those who truly want to discover or rekindle the life-giving power of the Holy Spirit in their everyday lives—at prayer, on the job, in school, in marriage and in the ordained and consecrated life of priests and religious.

Through sometimes delightful and always meaningful stories, Auntie Babsie demonstrates how the Holy Spirit calls us to conversion, gives us the gift of repentance and forms us as disciples of Jesus. She reminds us that without the Holy Spirit, there is no Christianity, no sacraments, no Scripture, no Church.

This book was written in response to the call of Pope John Paul II to prepare for the advent of the twenty-first century and Holy Year 2000. The Holy Father designated that in 1997 the Catholic Church was to reflect on Jesus, the Savior; in 1998, on the Holy Spirit; and in 1999, on God, the Father of Love. Each year is to be celebrated with a view to preparing for a new Pentecost, in which the Holy Spirit of God would fan our faith into a new flame that would enlighten the entire world.

Servant Publications asked Babsie to do this book for that specific reason—to help fan the new flame of that "new Pentecost." She approached this task with joy and quiet trust in God. I was truly honored when Auntie Babsie agreed to let me help her with this book. I know it will touch many people.

Jesus, in his last days on earth, both before and after his crucifixion and resurrection, promised to send the Advocate, the Holy Spirit who "will guide you to all truth." Jesus explained that the Holy Spirit "will not speak on his own, but he will speak what he hears, and will declare to you the things that are coming. He will glorify me, because he will take from what is mine and declare it to you" (Jn 16:13-14).

Auntie Babsie proclaims the fulfillment of Jesus' promise—the presence and power of the Spirit—in enthusiastic and utterly believable terms, for she speaks the simple language of faith. If you want to find peace of mind, joy of heart and union with your God, then this book is for you.

It is with great joy that I present to you Auntie Babsie.

Henry Libersat
Advent, 1996

Then afterward I will pour out
    my spirit upon all mankind.
Your sons and daughters shall prophesy,
    your old men shall dream dreams,
    your young men shall see visions;
Even upon the servants and the handmaids,
    in those days, I will pour out my spirit.

JOEL 3:1-2

CHAPTER ONE

A Journey of Faith Toward Jesus

I WAS NOT ALWAYS AWARE of the precious love God has for me and for all of us. There were times in my life when God seemed distant. Like many people, I suffered rejection, disappointment and disillusionment. Like too many people, I suffered divorce, not once but twice! I was a single parent, and raised two daughters on my own.

There were times when I did not realize how intimately God loves each one of us, how much he wants us to know him and to hear him when he speaks to us. As we will see later in these pages, the Holy Spirit utters our needs to the Father *even before we can express them.*

And God speaks to us. He speaks to us in words through revelation, and he speaks to us in the depths of our hearts. He wants us to understand what we hear. When God speaks, *he wants everybody to hear.* Everybody can hear, but the people who are equipped to understand his word are the members of his body—those who are signed and sealed with the Holy Spirit.

For all others, the Word creates a restlessness because they are striving to respond to something they do not understand and something they cannot interpret, but something they have heard—the Word. And the Word, unless interpreted and understood, disturbs.

I want to help people hear God calling. I hope to help people understand how they can grow in faith, how they can become more responsive to the Holy Spirit. Renewal of the Christian's life, and of the Church itself, means we must refresh our lives in the Spirit.

What is "life in the Spirit"? Living in the Spirit means to live as Jesus intends us to live. It means acknowledging the role of the Spirit in our lives, accepting his gifts and knowing they are meant for us, that they come to us a gift. Every Christian has gifts of the Spirit to make him holy and to help him help others. To live in the Spirit of God means to surrender oneself to our loving God for the sake of the kingdom of God.

It is the Holy Spirit who helps us to embrace God with a passionate desire to do his will, to become one with God and with all believers. To live in the Spirit is to experience the ultimate in freedom, joy, peace, love and security.

God works in mysterious ways, his wonders to behold! In my journey, he patiently and relentlessly led me to discover and become more open to the action of God's Holy Spirit in my life. He used the Cursillo movement and the charismatic renewal as his instruments. Others have grown in other ways. My own life has been so enriched by the lives and experiences of others who have shared their faith with me. To respond fully to the call of Christ is to grow in faith and to share faith with others, to help people come to know God and love him and serve him in this life, and to be happy with him forever in eternity.

When Pope John Paul II calls us to a "new evangelization" as we prepare for the Jubilee Year 2000, he is asking us to rediscover for ourselves the power of living under the influence of the Holy Spirit. What Christian can read the Acts of the Apostles and witness the powerful action of God in the lives of believers in the early Church, and come away unmoved? Oh, what a deep stirring and yearning those holy stories create in our hearts.

"Oh," our hearts cry, "if only we could witness that! If only we had been there! If only we could hear the Word preached with such power! If only we could see God's powerful intervention in our own day!"

Take heart! We can witness God's intervention in our own day. We have seen him in the wonderfully prophetic lives of modern saints such as Pope John Paul II, Mother Teresa and Father Solanus Casey.

Listen ... and God Will Speak to You

As you share the stories in these pages, you will see God's action in the world today. It can happen—and it does happen. It will happen to you, too.

"But, how can it happen to me?" you may ask. "I am not and do not want to be charismatic. I don't even know what a cursillo is. On the other hand, I truly desire to have a deeper personal relationship with God. I want to see and feel God's action in my life. How can I do it?"

Well, God works in our lives in different ways, but he is relentless in his pursuit of us and determined to draw us to himself for his own purpose. As you read these stories, reflect on your own life. If you feel a stirring and yearning in your heart, pray in faith for God to reveal himself to you. Pray fervently. Pray the Scriptures, don't just read them. Meditate on the great truths revealed by God and taught by the Church.

As you read the stories and thoughts in these pages, keep your Bible handy. Look up the references, meditate on them. Ask God to reveal to you what he wants you to know at that precise moment. He wrote the Scriptures for *you*—for you at this particular moment in time. He wrote the Scriptures so he could speak to your heart to teach, to comfort, to console and to lead you to life eternal with him.

God is timeless. He is eternal. But he reaches into time and lives in us and for us. If you ask God to help you, even if you consider yourself a stranger to a "life in the Spirit," even if you do not feel close to God, God will help you. Say to him, "Oh, God, speak to my heart. Help me to listen for your voice. I give myself to you. Hear me, dear Lord, and please answer me."

He will answer you. He *always* answers those who seek him with all their hearts.

Someone once said, "God writes straight in crooked lines." Maybe you have some "crooked lines" in your own life through which God is trying to speak to you. Reflect on these "lines" in your life as you share the experiences of others in these pages.

There surely have been crooked lines in our society—and God has used them to speak to us as a nation, as a community of human beings in the world. Let's look back, to the 1960s, when restlessness pervaded individual hearts, society, and even the Church. There we find Pope John XXIII leading the Church in prayer: "Come, Holy Spirit, renew your wonders in our time."

The Church at that time was restless, seeking its own identity, seeking to respond in a new way to God's call. At that time I, too, was restless, searching. I think my story will ring a familiar note in the hearts of many people, people who have searched, people who have suffered falsehood and even violence, people who have suffered the pain of failed marriages, people who have struggled to know the will of God in their own lives, and sought the strength to do God's will.

The Spirit in the Sixties

In the sixties, young people, stoned on drugs, tried to escape from the reality of a life they did not understand. They came together by the thousands and held big festivals. They heard the word "community," and they interpreted it as "communes." They heard the word "unity," and they came together, giving themselves to one another and striving to become one with one another.

And in the midst of it, the world looked on and laughed. The world thought these young people were completely off base, dropouts from society, living in a dream world.

But God did not laugh. God knows the hungers of the human heart. He made us and we belong to him. We are made in his image. We thirst for him, even when we seek meaning in life in the wrong direction. The minds and hearts of these mostly misguided youths were pointing to the need for a new spirit of love and unity. There were many in the Church that did not understand what was happening, did not sense the advent of a new season of Pentecost.

Thinking back on that time, I can't help but recall Jesus' triumphant entry into Jerusalem (Lk 19:28ff). Jesus had mounted the ass and was proceeding into Jerusalem, and ...

... the whole multitude of his disciples began to praise God aloud with joy for all the mighty deeds they had seen. They proclaimed:

> *"Blessed is the king who comes*
> *in the name of the Lord.*
> *Peace in heaven*
> *and glory in the highest!"*

Some of the Pharisees in the crowd said to him, "Teacher, rebuke your disciples." He said in reply, "I tell you, if they keep silent, the stones will cry out!"

In a way that is what happened. So many people who were Catholic never spoke the name of Jesus publicly, never shared their faith in him. And now, in the 1960s, from the stoned minds and heads of these young Jesus People, the name of Jesus became very public. It was as though the stones were crying out again. True, these Jesus People may have misunderstood Jesus. On Palm Sunday, many of the people who praised Jesus did not yet understand his mission. But Jesus accepted them where they were and he honored their praise.

So, it seems to me, it was with these Jesus People of the 1960s. They had risen up like mushrooms in the night—and in an instant they seemed to disappear. But the movement had produced a rich crop of men and women who had experienced a marvelous thing: The name of Jesus, which had been on their lips, had now entered into their hearts. These young people, and I met many of them, had come to know Jesus personally.

These men and women left their communes. Soon they were out on mission in various countries, making him known by gifts of song, gifts of music, mime, drama—whatever gifts they had. God was making himself known again through these young people and through the name of Jesus. God surely works in mysterious ways!

The Language of the Spirit

The Spirit was speaking his language of love to the Catholic Church at that time, too. It has always been that way. God speaks to all, because God is a lover of all people, and he wants to give everybody a chance. But only those who are his children, his family, those who know the language of the family, can interpret what he is saying.

I have two daughters, and as with all parents and children, we had our own "language." There were certain words my little daughters used, and only the family knew what they meant. In their baby talk, they always asked for "rocamoni." They could not say "macaroni" until they were big enough to read. When they wanted sardines, they asked for "amon." And when they wanted to eat pig tails, my little daughters would ask for "rolled up fat."

Any stranger coming into the house would be hard put to attend to my daughters' needs because their vocabulary would not be understood. But we understood, and at their first whisper we attended to them and let them have what they wanted.

So it is with the family of God. Even when we do not pray or do not know how to pray, God knows our needs, hears our hearts and loves us. He understands our groping ways and inadequate language, especially when we speak of loving him and needing him.

At the same time, because we are the Church formed and filled with the Holy Spirit, we have a dynamic vocabulary that helps us to interpret the Word of God according to the mind of God, and not according to our own fancy. And, even when we do not hear well, God finds ways to open our ears and our eyes.

In the 1960s, the people in the Church had largely forgotten how to hear God's call. We were praying in the Church's own language, true, but we were no longer attentive to the voice of the Spirit. The people in the Church had become almost "fossilized" in their response to the faith. They believed nothing in the Church could ever change since truth never changes. Our faith was expressed uniformly; we had become both sacramentalized and ritualized. There is certainly nothing wrong with sacrament and ritual, but the power of our sacramental faith had become camouflaged with comfortable sameness. God was a distant mystery instead of a dynamic, intimate Father and Savior.

There was great consolation in the routine and rhythm of our faith. In spite of the sameness, the faith was far from dead. Though it might not have seemed dynamic, it was steadfast. At this point in history, John XXIII recognized and heard the voice of the Spirit, and realized that God wanted to "renew the face of the earth."

The Holy Father heard the message and captured it, but he knew he could not do it alone, so he got the whole Church praying. This is the prayer we prayed, the prayer of Pope John XXIII as he called together that momentous gift of God, the Second Vatican Council:

O Holy Spirit, sent by the Father in the name of Jesus, who art present in the Church and dost infallibly guide it, pour forth, we pray, the fullness of Thy gifts upon the Ecumenical Council.

Enlighten, O most gracious Teacher and Comforter, the minds of our prelates who, in prompt response to the Supreme Roman Pontiff, will carry on the sessions of the Sacred Council.

Grant that from this Council abundant fruit may ripen; that the light and strength of the gospel may be extended more and more in human society; that the Catholic religion and its active missionary work may flourish with ever greater vigor, with the happy result that knowledge of the Church's teaching may spread and Christian morality have a salutary increase.

O sweet Guest of the soul, strengthen our minds in the truth and dispose our hearts to pay reverential heed, that we may accept with sincere submission those things which shall be decided in the Council and fulfill them with ready will.

We pray for those sheep who are not now of the one fold of Jesus Christ, that even as they glory in the name of Christian, they may come at last to unity under the governance of the one Shepherd.

Renew Thy wonders in this our day, as by a new Pentecost. Grant to Thy Church that, being of one mind and steadfast in prayer with Mary, the Mother of Jesus, and following the lead of Blessed Peter, it may advance the reign of our Divine Savior, the reign of truth and justice, the reign of love and peace. Amen.[1]

Many people prayed this prayer, without understanding what it was all about. They prayed it out of obedience. I was among those who prayed this prayer every day. Every time I prayed it, I asked myself what a "new Pentecost" would be like. Many times, I went back and read the story of Pentecost (see Acts 1 and 2) and wondered whether it was possible that we could see these times again.

Was it possible that God's Word could be preached with such power that thousands would be converted on the spot? Was it possible that, in our time, we could have the gift of tongues so that our preaching would be heard and understood by the peoples of various nations and languages?

In time God answered my questions. But at that time I was not yet ready for those answers.

Babsie's Search for the Spirit

I had been brought up as a Catholic: I was taught by Irish nuns, received the sacraments from Irish priests and confirmed by an Irish bishop. I knew the little *Baltimore Catechism* by heart. I was always striving to live it, because the Irish nuns had assured me I could get to heaven that way.

I grew up reading the lives of the saints, never believing I could *be* a saint because I had never seen a black one. I thought about being a nun, but again, I had never seen a black nun, so I very soon concluded that religious life was not for black people. Nobody told me this, and I never asked anyone. I just decided myself that black people could not become sisters or priests. But I knew I could get to heaven, and I knew that God loved all people of all races and all tongues. The Irish nuns had laid that foundation very deeply.

At that time, the slogan was, "Little children must be seen and not heard." So all the questions remained in our minds because nobody taught us how to ask God questions. We asked

God for things we wanted, but were not so conversant with God that we could reveal our hearts and expect him to answer.

All avenues, save marriage, seemed closed to me. So I got married, and the next nineteen years were a searching, painful, floundering passage from bad to unbearable—from escape to the brink of suicide. During that nineteen years, my first husband and I divorced. Eight years after my first divorce, I remarried outside the Church. That was a mistake. I finally realized I was putting my soul in jeopardy, and my husband's as well, so we separated and ended our marriage.

I had never stopped going to Mass after my first divorce and remarriage, but, of course, I had not been receiving communion. I longed to be reconciled with God and with the Church. After leaving my second husband, I went to confession, was reconciled and began again to be active in the Church. I became so deeply involved in a life of prayer and searching for God that I lost all desire to marry again. (My first husband is now dead. My second became reconciled with the Church and is an active lay minister.)

Because of my background in a strong Catholic family in which marriages always succeeded, I had thought mine would also. So I suffered intense pain, guilt, and humiliation when I found myself divorced.

My first marriage and divorce were a source of great embarrassment for me and my family. In my country, Trinidad, a divorce is a disaster. Divorce was held in such disdain that my father was told by our parish priest, "I am questioning whether I should allow you to receive the sacraments because you are harboring a divorcée." And my father came home perplexed and sad. But he was not angry. When he told us what had happened, I was consumed with pain.

I had to make a public apology for the scandal I had caused by my divorce, and I had to put it in the newspaper. I struggled with this shame, not angry with anyone but myself. I was very angry with myself. But my family absorbed me and supported me.

So, in the 1960s, I was twice married and twice divorced, and I had my two daughters from the first marriage. I had to bring up these two children as a single mother, but I had the full support of my natural family. I had a good job, working as a secretary in management for a major oil company. I was good at my job, and eventually I was head of a large stenographic pool. In time I was elected to political office, and I tried to do what I could to bring about racial harmony among the different ethnic groups in my country.

This period was very difficult for me. There was racial unrest in the country between the two predominant races—African and East Indian—that up to then had lived so well together. When I was elected to office, I worked to bring together the diverse groups of people who inhabited my country: Africans and East Indians, those of French and Spanish origin, as well as the English and Irish and those descended from the native Carib Indians indigenous to the islands. (I have African, Carib, French and Spanish blood flowing in my own veins, and I have always tried to claim the strongest characteristics of those peoples.)

I felt the call to do everything in my power to preserve the unity and respect among the African and East Indian races. So I joined the political party that was predominantly East Indian just because I wanted to make a statement. I knew—we all knew—that the country was too small to risk racial war. We had seen what happened in Ghana, and the last thing in the world I wanted to see was that terrible ordeal in Trinidad. So out of love for God, out of a response which I thought God wanted and a desire to heal the relationship between the races, I joined the party—and became myself the object of anger.

During the next election I saw people as I had never seen them before, and had never guessed they could be. It was a real revelation; some of my own relatives, my own friends, and, what was most painful of all, other Catholics turned against me. The anger was so great that there was real danger. I remember one time in particular when the police had to surround me, had to protect me with their own bodies from the crowds. Even then, some women were screaming and pushing to hit me over the shoulders of the police officers.

I lost the election, and my party became the opposition party. The party sued the government for immoral practices, for lying during the election. Again, "Bleasdell" was all over the papers. It was like "Bleasdell Against the Government." My name was all over. Even taxi drivers and street cleaners were talking about me. It was a trying time. Twice, now, had I become notorious—through divorce and now in politics. Both were very painful times.

Nevertheless, I came out alive and really questioning what God was all about. Was he real? Did he really care? Did it make any real difference whether you were Christian or Muslim or Hindu? I felt a need to seek God with all my heart. In the midst of it all, I still held on to the prayer of John XXIII, *"Renew your wonders in our time, as by a new Pentecost."*

And just when I thought the answers would never come, God spoke to me in a dream.

"Child, You Have a Big, Big Grace."

In our culture, dreams are important, not just, as one psychologist said, a way in which our minds try to interpret sensations experienced in sleep. God speaks through dreams. He did so with Jacob, St. Joseph, and many others.

The dream came in the eight years between my first divorce and my second marriage. During this time, I was angry and full of pain and shame. I was living with my parents with my two children. As was the custom, my youngest sister had married and moved in with our parents, to care for them. My sister soon had two children. I knew I had to find a place of my own, which again was unheard of, a woman living on her own without family. I began to pray for a house. And in the midst of this, my father died. It was a very difficult time, but a time in which I had continued my search for God.

It was then I had the dream. I dreamed I was coming out of a church. In front of the church was a long driveway to the street. In the street was a large procession of people, innumerable people, and they were marching along. They just filled the street, shoulder to shoulder, marching along. It was clear they belonged to each other. They had a set purpose.

I stood on the steps of the church and wondered where all these people were going. "Surely they couldn't be coming here, to the church," I said to myself. "This is my parish. If something were going on, the priest would have announced it and I would know what was going on." I took the driveway toward the street, intending to leave, but the procession turned into the driveway from the street. I couldn't believe the masses and masses of people coming to the church. So I stepped on the curb to give them room to pass. They filled the whole driveway coming up. As they passed me, I turned around, really in awe, and I said, "I don't believe this, I really don't believe this. Where are all these people going?"

And out of the corner of my eye, I spotted a grotto which I hadn't noticed before. Our Lady's eyes were also riveted on these people as they went. So, I looked at her and she was very serious and very sad. I said, "Mother of God, you're sad." She turned and looked at me, and her eyes were purple with pain. She stared at me and I said, "You are sad because they are passing you straight. Never mind, never mind, Mother of God, I will never pass you straight. I will always, always stop and talk to you. Will you smile for me, Mother of God?"

And she looked at me as though she could see my soul, piercingly, and she smiled, with her lips, but her eyes didn't change.

And I said to her, "Just one smile, Mother of God, just one little smile." And she looked at me again, searchingly, and then her eyes picked up the smile. It seemed to me she now smiled from her heart. I fell on my knees and said, "Mother of God, will you please bless me?" She lifted her right hand over me and from her fingers came drops of blood and water and they glistened as they fell on my head and on my face. I said, "Thank you, Mother of God," and then I woke up.

The next morning I got up and told my mother about the dream. She looked at me and she said, "Child, you got a big grace. You got a big, big grace." I turned away thinking, "What's a grace?"

Two weeks later, I found a house. I asked my younger brother to move in with me, to have a male figure in the house for my children. He agreed. The next day, my mother said I should talk to my godmother. I went to my godmother who lived in the heart of the town. She said she knew I had found a house to rent but if I wanted to start a household of my own, why didn't I think of taking her house? She gave me her house as a gift. We would make it comfortable, and she would live with me. She was going blind very fast. So this is what we did. We settled as a family—my brother, godmother, my two children and me.

Later, it occurred to me that this house was the grace, the gift Our Lady gave to me. So I decided to call the house Ave Maria. However, it would be many years before I fully understood the dream.

After the children were grown and settled in Canada, I decided to resign my job with the oil company and take some time off to pray, to search. By that time I was reading everything, everything, everything I could read. In my reading, I learned that Mahatma Gandhi said he read the Bible and the life of Christ. He was so impressed with Christ that he wanted to be a Christian, but he had met too many Christians. I began to search my own heart. Had Gandhi met me, would he have had a different opinion of Christians? I wasn't sure.

The Charismatic Renewal and Vatican II

In spite of all the personal difficulties I had encountered up to that time, I knew that I wanted to follow Christ. On the other hand, it was not easy to be Catholic. It may be hard for younger Catholics to understand the trauma we experienced during and after Vatican Council II. But, by understanding what we went through, younger Catholics may be better able to understand the challenges we all face today.

During all my personal difficulties with divorce and public anger, the changes of Vatican II were beginning to take place in the Church. Latin was out, and the vernacular was in. The altar was turned around. Out went the statues of the saints. Out went all the old hymns we knew, and in came some very Protestant-sounding ones. The organ was silent and guitars made their debut. But, for me, the most difficult thing of all was the sign of peace. I had been taught all my life to keep quiet in church. The sisters used to poke me in the back and say, "Keep your eyes on the altar. That's where you must look. Be quiet. Don't talk." And when the sisters were not there, my mother took over poking me in the back and saying, "Keep your eyes on the altar. Be quiet. Don't talk. "

And now, the priest was telling me to turn away from the altar, open my mouth and talk to people: "The peace of Christ be with you."

The questions filled my mind: *If English is now okay in the Mass, why did we have to learn Latin when we were five? If the organ is not so holy, why have we not always had guitars? Why? Why? Why?* I experienced a deep, spiritual restlessness.

The confusion was endless. The changes had come upon us without explanation or preparation. They just happened. But because we were Catholic to our very cores, there was no place else we could go. We kept on persevering, asking questions of each other and not realizing, in our own bewilderment, that the priests and nuns were also going through crises and whatever they were doing for renewal was only an obedient response to the pope and the bishops.

In the midst of all this I found a prayer to the Holy Spirit, a prayer composed and recommended by Cardinal Mercier of Belgium. In presenting this prayer to the Church, Cardinal Mercier said he was going to reveal to us "a secret of sanctity and happiness." He said our lives will "pass happily" if for five minutes every day we keep our imaginations quiet, shut our eyes "to all the things of sense" and close our ears "to all the sounds of earth." He said by doing this we would "withdraw into the sanctuary of your baptized soul, which is the temple of the Holy Spirit." When in that place, that sanctuary, he said we should pray this prayer:

Holy Spirit, soul of my soul, I adore Thee. Enlighten, guide, strengthen and console me; tell me what I ought to do and command me to do it. I promise to be submissive in everything that Thou shalt ask of me and to accept all that Thou permittest to happen to me. Only show me what is Thy will.

"If you do this," Cardinal Mercier promised, "your life will pass happily and serenely, consolation will abound even in the midst of troubles, for grace will be given in proportion to the trial, as well as strength to bear it, bringing you to the gates of paradise full of merit. This submission to the Holy Spirit is the secret of sanctity."

I distributed this prayer all over the world, and I have added my own thought: "The Holy Spirit, the Breath of God that unites the Father and the Son, is the Giver of all gifts, the Sanctifier of all graces. It is difficult to comprehend why his help is not invoked more consistently by those who wish to be witnesses to Christ. The Holy Spirit helps us, despite opposition, to prove Christianity to a sinful world."

When I found Cardinal Mercier's prayer, I began to pray it

continuously. I was so much in need. I had the sense that, since we were all so disturbed, if we prayed together and spoke to God, rehearsed our pain in the ear of God in each other's presence, God would answer. My own impassioned plea to God was, "If you are real, come to our help—or forever keep your peace." And that was the attitude with which, finally, thirty of us sat down to pray in our home.

The Beginnings of a New Life in Prayer

Little did we know what God had planned for us, and how this searching and praying would lead us into the beauties and mysteries of lives lived in the Holy Spirit. I want to share these early days with you. It may help you understand how we grew in awareness of the action of the Holy Spirit—and, in that understanding, you may find it easier today, on the threshold of the new millennium, to recognize how the Spirit of God is reaching out to you.

Among us, in our new prayer group, was a young seminarian, Harcourt Blackett, who had been a Protestant. After conversion as an adult, he went into the seminary. He was to become, ultimately, like a son to me, a priest to serve our little community, our dear Father Michael Moses.

Harcourt was precious to our new prayer group. He knew the Scriptures, and he also was very comfortable with spontaneous prayer. He led us in prayer and in song. He had a beautiful voice.

For some, the atmosphere, with all the singing and Scripture reading, seemed too Protestant and they left. The few of us remained, and people came and went. We prayed like that for six months.

At end of the six months, on March 23, 1971, the local seminary invited Dr. Josephine Massyngbaerde-Ford to talk to the seminarians about a new phenomenon, the charismatic renewal. They invited us, and the other two prayer groups in the country, to attend the lecture. One was made up of the privileged people, mostly white; the group originated from A Better World Retreat; the second group, which met in the cloistered Dominican convent, was made up of the ordinary poor folks in our town, Arima. We were all brought together because of our connection to the seminary through Harcourt. It was there that we discovered the charismatic renewal.

Father Duffy's Prophetic Word

The charismatic renewal is a spiritual movement that made its debut in the Church in 1967, shortly after Vatican Council II ended. It is a movement that helps people accept the gifts of the Holy Spirit received in baptism and confirmation. It also helps people to open themselves to other gifts which St. Paul mentions in 1 Corinthians. We'll go into all these gifts later.

But the charismatic renewal finds its roots in the very first Pentecost and in the powerful witness of the apostolic Church. Since 1967, it has swept through the Church, embraced enthusiastically by some and rejected just as enthusiastically by others.

Some people do not understand this renewal movement, or have had bad experiences because of a few people who have given it a bad name. Many do not realize that the charismatic renewal movement was approved by Pope Paul VI himself, and has received the support of bishops from around the world. In 1975 the pope himself attended an international gathering of the charismatic renewal in Rome. On that occasion, in comments to the thousand of Catholics from throughout the world, he thanked the renewal for "coming to Rome to teach us how to praise."

So, yes, I was and am a part of this Spirit-filled movement. But I am also a traditional Catholic who embraces all the traditional devotions and disciplines of our Holy Church. And I hope, dear reader, regardless of what you think about charismatics or traditionalists, that what follows in all these pages will convince you of God's love for you and his desire to transform us and to use us to build up his kingdom.

One year and one month after this gathering at the seminary, a priest from the Madonna House Apostolate, Father James Duffy (another Irishman), came to sit in at our meeting one night. The night he came, my sister also came to the meeting. She was a very good Catholic, very confident of her Catholic faith. She had always had precarious health. Her life was prayer. She had a dependence on God and the ability to say, "Thy will be done."

That night, she was violently ill. She had just gone through surgery. We had picked her up and carried her to the prayer meeting. After an hour, with Father saying nothing and me leading the meeting because Harcourt wasn't there that night, my sister said she was in a lot of pain and had to go home.

After she left, Father Duffy asked who she was, and I said, "My sister."

He said, "God wanted to heal her but you didn't pray." We didn't know about praying for healing. He said, "There is a beautiful gift of prayer in this room, and a lot of other gifts besides; if you don't recognize them and use them they will dry up." He asked me, "Would you allow me to use you as proxy to pray for your sister?"

I said, "Father, you can do anything you want," and I immediately knelt down.

He gathered all the people around. He said, "The united faith in this room will heal that woman. God wants to heal her. Let us pray. Never mind what I am doing, you pray for all you're worth, keeping your mind on the fact that we are praying for her healing."

He laid hands on me and told everyone to touch one another. He began to pray, and that night we most surely experienced praying in tongues and the gift of prophecy. It was a most amazing experience. I mention these events because the Holy Spirit does indeed have gifts for us, and he wants us to use them to build up the Church.

That night, Father Duffy spoke a prophetic word over me:

I have loved you with an everlasting love and I am constant in my affection for you. When you were conceived in your mother's womb I beheld you. And I have loved you with an infinite love. I have selected you and set you apart for a work that you must do for me. For this purpose have I continually defended you against lying tongues and against tigers' teeth that would have destroyed you. Have I not constantly defended you and protected you and brought you to this hour?

As he was speaking these words over me, I saw my whole life pass before me. I realized that all my life, from the age of six, I had been surrounded with contentions. People had told lies about me many, many times and I could never understand that. So when God asked me, through Father Duffy's prophetic word, "Have I not continually defended you against lying tongues and against tigers' teeth?" the whole thing came back. I began to weep, to sob and sob. My heart cried out, "Lord, you saw all of it. You knew they were lying about me and in the midst of all this you loved me still! Then what have I got to fear? If you know me and you love me, I have nothing to fear." A whole sense of tremendous liberation came over me as I wept and wept. I couldn't stop weeping.

Then Father Duffy put his hand on me and began to pray a prayer of peace. I can still hear him, "I impart the peace of Christ to you, my daughter. Peace that surpasses understanding. I bring you peace that the world cannot give and the world cannot take away. Peace be with you. Receive the peace."

He took my hand and lifted me up. He said that God had chosen me for a special work but I had to fast and pray much.

The next morning, I woke up with a sense of tremendous joy and an assurance that everything would be all right. I went to see my sister and found her completely well. God had healed her. After three months of severe illness in which she couldn't do anything, she was able to resume work.

After reflection, I realized that the night before I had seen the gifts of the Spirit in full operation. It was an answer to the prayer we had prayed with John XXIII during the council: *"Renew your wonders in this our day, as by a new Pentecost...."*

I had wondered whether God would answer that prayer, and if he did, what it would be like. I had not realized that in Vatican II, the answer to the prayer was inherent. We had been resisting all the changes, not realizing that they were preparatory for the new Pentecost for which we had prayed.

From this point, I was sensitive to gifts. I realized that in me, in this new life in the Spirit, his gifts had been stirred up. And the fruits of the Spirit were evident—joy and peace and kindness. This priest had exercised several gifts: tongues, interpretation of tongues, knowledge (he knew God wanted to heal my sister), discernment (he recognized there was a gift of prayer and other gifts in our meeting), wisdom (he knew God wanted to heal and he knew what to do to facilitate the healing), healing and prophecy. (I will indeed go more into detail about the gifts and fruit of the Spirit.)

Later, Father Duffy sought me out. He said that as he spoke God's word over me, he was never more certain that it was indeed God giving him a prophetic word. He wanted to talk with me. After speaking with Father, I decided I would do what God asked, pray and fast much.

Questions for Reflection

1. Have you ever felt hatred or prejudice? If so, how did you deal with those feelings? After reading this first chapter, do you have any helpful insights into prejudice and division?

2. If you have had a deeply moving spiritual experience, how does it compare with Auntie Babsie's? Share with a loved one, or your spiritual director, how that experience changed you or what it meant to you.

3. Have you ever heard God speak to your heart? How did it affect you?

1. *Documents of Vatican II*, Walter M. Abbott, S.J. ed. (New York: The America Press, 1966), 793.

CHAPTER TWO

The Spirit Enlivens
the Church

WHAT BEGAN AS MY OWN QUEST FOR TRUTH and a prayer group for our own sakes became an influence in the whole country. It seemed that, in the renewal of the spirit of Catholic laity in the charismatic renewal, all roads led to Arima. However, we were soon to learn that the same movement was spreading rapidly throughout the Church in many nations.

People were coming from all the towns and the farthest points in the country to Arima. They were coming to see what was happening, what God was doing. We found the house overflowing. People were standing outside in the yard and in the street to take part in the prayer meetings.

Jesus, through the Holy Spirit, was drawing people together, so we could come to terms with who we were as Catholics called to renewal by the Vatican Council II. We were being called to be witnesses wherever we were. We were learning that we had to make a commitment to Jesus who was the Lord and center of our lives.

Soon, the gathering was so large we had to seek the help of the Dominican Fathers, who gave us use of the chapel, which could accommodate about five hundred people. Under the umbrella of the Dominican Fathers, we earned credibility. It was amazing. All the races of the country were coming together to pray and to seek the face of God. The Church began to come alive. A sleeping giant, the Catholic laity, was awakening in the Church. Over time, with Father Duffy, the movement has moved to the other Caribbean Islands. All these islands and countries became involved in the renewal and looked to Trinidad for leadership.

People were showing a desire for unity and community. People were taking responsibility in their parish churches. Catholics, with renewed faith through Life in the Spirit seminars, had become lay ministers in their parishes. They were eucharistic ministers, lectors and teachers of religion. They were the ones who enthusiastically embraced these ministries. They sang in the choirs. Church attendance increased, congregational singing improved dramatically. They were members of this renewal in the Spirit that came forth answering the call of Vatican II for lay people to become involved in their Church.

We began to see that every movement in the Church needed to be invigorated by the Spirit. We began to see that part of our call was to give Life in the Spirit seminars to each movement in the Church. The Life in the Spirit seminar helps believers discover more deeply God's unconditional love for them, helps them open up to that love, introduces them more intimately to the gifts of the Holy Spirit received at baptism and confirmation and invites them, through prayer, to receive the fullness of the Spirit in their lives.

The Cursillo movement prepared me for the work God had for me, namely, to be an instrument through which the charismatic renewal could begin in Trinidad and throughout the

Caribbean. All the experiences of my life, even those resulting from bad decisions which led to abuse from others, were used by God to prepare me for the work I was called to do. I came to understand what St. Theresa meant when she said whether she is praised or abused made no difference to her. What she was trying to do was please God. Just as God helped her, so he would help me to persevere, to keep my eyes on him and his perfect will, whether there was praise or blame from others.

For me personally, it was a time of discovery of God's will for me. It became clear through prayer that God wanted to use me as a teacher in this movement for spiritual renewal through the Holy Spirit. I complained to God that I did not know enough to teach, but God let me know in my heart that he would guide me, teach me and help me teach others.

That call to teach, and the firm assurance that God was with me, reminded me of the Annunciation when Mary was asked to be the Mother of Jesus. Mary said, "But I can't. I don't have a husband."

And the angel told her, "Never mind, the Holy Spirit will come upon you and power from the Most High will over-shadow you and that which will be born of you will be called holy, Son of God, Savior of the world."

I came to realize that God himself calls, and if we hear the call he enables us. In his very call is his enabling power. And as Father Duffy had said the night he prayed over me, "If God calls you, he enables you." So God was telling me all he needed from me was consent and he would enable me.

I mention this again because it is so important for Catholics and all Christians to realize *that God does work in our lives, does call us to do things that seem beyond our abilities, things that are new and were never part of our plans for our lives.* Who would have thought that a modest little virgin would become the mother of the Savior of the world? Who would think that a woman, twice divorced, a woman who had been scorned by society and a source of division among the people she had sought to unify, could be called by God to help renew his Church through the power of the Holy Spirit?

God who begins a good work in us can bring it to completion. God himself, St. Paul says, is the author and finisher of our faith. *We have the freedom to say yes or no. Once we have given that "yes" to God, he will never forsake us.* He will continue to enable us as we look to him as the source of power and of life.

Eventually there were more than a hundred prayer groups in the country, and we thought of having a rally that would bring us all together to celebrate our faith and the work God had done in our lives. So, in January of 1976, more than five thousand people came together in the biggest place available—the horse racing track. We gathered together in the power of the Spirit, singing praise to God, singing in tongues. There were three bishops from three Caribbean islands and thirty priests present. It was a glorious day. All you could do was look at it and say, "See what God has done!"

And God had done a wonder in our lives. But he had an added gift for us. In fact, although it was a spiritually glorious day, the weather was very bad. Rain came, and people began to run for shelter because half the stands were uncovered. I was led to say, by the Spirit, "Christians! Don't run! Stand up. God has given us authority over the work of his hands. Let's stand up and talk to the weather in Jesus' name."

The people heard the call and stopped. I spoke to the weather in the name of Jesus—but the rain just poured down in torrents and the people ran away again. I was dripping wet. My shoes had a half inch of water in them. So I thought, "Well, everybody's gone, so I might as well go, too. God will not hear this prayer."

But *then I saw three young men sitting in that torrential downpour, hands upraised, dripping wet, and they represented three of the races of our country—an African, an Indian, and a Portuguese.* There they were, glistening with rain, eyes closed. They reminded me of Shadrach, Meshach, and Abednego (see Dn 3).

I turned again to the Lord and I said, "Lord if you cannot do it for me, for the sake of the faith of these three young men, will you please do it? You did it for Joshua, you can do it for me." So I prayed, "Let the clouds be parted in Jesus name." And BOOM, the clouds opened up and a ray of sunshine fell upon us. And the whole five thousand people shouted exultantly. They couldn't stop shouting.

The rest of the day, God protected us. The rain fell everywhere, but it was as though we were covered by a great bowl. Everybody looked at the rain and marveled at what God could do. We knew we were enjoying God's favor in a very real way.

Being human, some of us began to worry that the rain would again come upon us, but one man said, "When God has acted, don't let the symptoms confuse you." That has become for me a watchword, *"When God has acted, don't let the symptoms confuse you."* When God has acted, God will stand by his own actions no matter what it seems is happening everywhere; you just hold onto the faith that God has acted. No one can undo what God has done.

There was still another lesson to learn. After this marvelous experience of God's power, division set in among the national leaders. I began to see the word of Josephine Massyngbaerde-Ford come into reality: *Gifts divide, fruit unites.*

Jealousy had set in among us. People envied one another's gifts rather than rejoice in the fact that God so blesses his Church. I knew we had to come to terms with the gifts of the Spirit, recognize those gifts in one another and free one another to exercise those gifts. I began to pray over this problem.

Lent came. We were fasting and praying, each one in his own prison. It was like a spiritual desolation. During Holy Week we asked the priest if he would leave the Blessed Sacrament exposed all during Easter week. He agreed and we took turns praying all that week. I would go home for a while and return. I was desolated. It seemed all darkness. I cried out to God, "Where are you? It's so dark. My present state is worse than the first. I was in the light and now it is so dark. This darkness is untenable! I can't stand it! Where are you?"

On Wednesday of Easter week, I felt the presence of the Lord so strongly that I stood dead still where I was. The Lord spoke. He said, "I have caused you to live out in your flesh my message for my people today. *Tell my people unless they use to the fullest the wind of the Spirit now blowing, their last state will be worse than the first.*" The message was so clear that I wrote it down. The minute I received the word and wrote it down the darkness lifted. It was like a barrier had been removed. I had been given a message and I felt it was for the whole renewal. Indeed, the message may well serve the whole Church.

Questions for Reflection

1. "If God calls you, he enables you." When was the last time you experienced God giving you strength to do something that was very difficult for you?
2. Babsie observes that the "gifts divide, but fruit unites." What does this say about the qualities that are most important in a person who wants to serve God?
3. Have you ever felt abandoned by God? What happened? And what did you learn from the experience?

CHAPTER THREE

In Search of the Gifts
of the Spirit

THERE IS SO MUCH TO KNOW about the Holy Spirit! How impoverished we remain if we do not seek to know, understand and receive the Spirit of God!

What God has done for many people through spiritual renewal movements, God wants for his entire Church. How many people have discovered the power of God in their lives through Cursillo, Marriage Encounter and the charismatic renewal—to name only a few! How God longs to see his entire Church refreshed and renewed in the Spirit.

Learning to Move in the Gifts of the Spirit

Pentecost was not for the Apostolic Church only. Pentecost is for us today; it happens today through baptism and confirmation—and is made evident in a special way when people discover the power of the Spirit and surrender their lives to him. The Spirit blows where he will and he expresses his power in different people and situations in different ways. A large number of Catholics were to learn more about the Holy Spirit and experience a special manifestation of the Spirit through a Pentecostal woman of great faith.

Through an unusual series of events, we learned about Mary Goddard, a wonderful Pentecostal lady known for her teachings on the gifts of the Spirit. She had taught in convents and churches in Malaysia and Singapore with great results; the bishops of those countries were willing to recommend her to teach Catholics. And she was due to visit Trinidad.

When she came, the priests and lay leaders met with Mary to discern whether she should be "unleashed" on the Catholic flock. We discovered she had a great love for Catholics and she was open to Christian unity. She would consider it a deep privilege to teach. She loved Catholics because she found them hungry for the Word of God.

She began to prophesy over the leaders of the renewal in a manner we had never heard before. She prophesied over priests and leaders with such excitement that we knew she was a gift from God.

The end result was that she taught us for a full week, seven days from eight in the morning to ten at night, teaching us about the gifts of the Holy Spirit. Her course usually took seven weeks. She said to condense it into one week would take a miracle—but she was open to miracles.

She did it. Four hundred and fifty people from the prayer groups—leaders and members of their core groups—attended the weeklong seminar. Mary lectured five one-hour sessions on the gift of tongues. She lectured on prophecy and all the other Corinthian gifts: wisdom in discourse, the power to express knowledge, faith, healing, miraculous powers, discernment and interpretation of tongues. Through this experience we saw a movement of the Spirit nobody could have imagined! In one of the meetings, all four hundred fifty people, priests and all, were blessed with a deep anointing of the Spirit.

At the end of that week, people went off with a knowledge of gifts and with the determination to discern who had gifts and how to use those gifts and to rejoice in them. Mary had convinced us that gifts were to be sought after. She read from 1 Corinthians 14, in which St. Paul urges us to know and seek the gifts of the Spirit. *"If you desire a gift, ask for it. God wants you to ask."* Her teaching blew away the whole Catholic attitude that "if God wants me to have a gift he'll give it to me—I don't have to ask."

God wants to give us all the gifts. They are for us, for the Church. The gifts enable us to witness to the presence, power and love of God. He creates in us the desire, the will and the accomplishment. When he quickens our wills to ask for gifts, we should take it for granted that it is God who initiated the desire in us and he was hoping we would say "yes" and put out our hands to receive them.

To ask God for a gift is not a sign of pride but one of deep faith and humility. And when someone has a gift, it is a cause for rejoicing because these ministerial gifts are not for ourselves but for others, for the community. They free us to be ministers of God. When a person receives a gift, the community is gifted.

The Unifying Gift of the Spirit

Mary Goddard stayed with us ten weeks, and during that time we took her to the other islands, both the Dutch and English islands. The whole Caribbean was becoming united in the Spirit. What politicians had tried to do for many, many years and failed, now the Church, by the power of the Spirit, was achieving! There was a spirit of unity among the various Caribbean islands. What man had failed to do God was able to do—and did—through the movement of the Holy Spirit!

This account of the power of the Spirit to unite his Church through his gifts is important as a reflection for this present day. There is so much suffering and division in both the Church and the world. If Catholics and other Christians would only surrender their lives to God, search for his will, accept the Spirit's gifts and obey his promptings, the face of the earth and the life of the Church would dramatically change!

The faithful people of God, open to the promptings, guidance and gifts of the Spirit, can indeed bring light, healing and peace to the world.

Say "Yes" to God's Gifts

It is not easy, at times, to say "yes" to a gift. Having a gift is a responsibility. You must use it for others. Let me explain by telling you what happened to me. A year after Mary's classes, she came back to speak at a conference in Trinidad. While Mary was praying for people, I stood by her. A woman approached me with her child, a twelve-year-old girl, who was screaming and screaming. The woman told me, "I want you to pray for her."

I said, "Let Mary pray for her." She said, "No, I want you to pray for her."

I said to myself, "Lord, what am I to do? I don't know what to do!" Then I asked the mother, "Why is your child screaming?"

And she replied, "Never mind that, she's just afraid of the crowd. Just pray for her." I asked her what was wrong with the child and she said the child could not speak.

So I laid hands on the child's throat and I spoke to her vocal cords in the name of Jesus, asking Jesus to heal her. Then I prayed for peace for the child and her screaming subsided.

The next day, Mary and I left the country. When I returned, I went to the cathedral to pray. The mother had been searching for me and found me there. I asked, "How is your child?"

She said, "The child speaks!" She said she had a gift for me and wanted to bring the little girl to see me. I said I had no need for a gift but I would happily see the child.

She came to my house with the child, and when the child saw me, she shouted, "Babsie!" I was surprised at first. I mean, in my country children are taught to address their elders with respect; even old people call me "Auntie Babsie." And this child called me "Babsie!" Laughing, I said to the child, "You have the right to call me Babsie!" I was humbled to realize that through this little child God had taught me to be open to his gift of healing.

The Gift of Knowledge

I was to learn much more from this beautiful Canadian Pentecostal woman. One lesson stays vividly in mind. It was a lesson about the gift of knowledge. She said that in this gift, the Lord will reveal to you something that it is impossible for you to know naturally. So it has to be through the inspiration of the Holy Spirit.

We were at a large teaching session in south Trinidad. I had gone there in extreme pain. It isn't very dignified, but I have to tell you, I had a severe attack of hemorrhoids. Nobody knew. It was so bad it was like I was eating pain day and night. As I was helping to support people in prayer, this man said, "I have a strange thing to say. I am ashamed and embarrassed to say it." I asked him what it was. He said, "Somebody in here is suffering with hemorrhoids." I laughed in surprise and said in jest, "Gee, you didn't have to take my pants down in public!" At this, the poor man blushed and he said I should get Mary to pray. Mary said to the man, "No, it's your word of knowledge. God will give you the power to pray."

I said to him, "Come on, now. You can't let me down. You've stimulated my hope that I could get some relief from my pain." I suffered with this affliction from time to time. It would just come upon me. As embarrassed as he was, he prayed with me. From that day in 1978 to this very day I have never had another attack. Immediately I got relief and it has never returned.

God used this man, as embarrassed as he was and as incompetent as he felt. God gave him the word of knowledge and heard his prayer to give me a permanent healing. That's what can happen when people put their faith in God, their expectant faith. *God can use anyone, and he often chooses the simple to confound the wise.*

Generally, when people have such a healing gift, they seem to be confident in themselves. But something happened that same night that surprised even Mary. The Holy Spirit touched more than four hundred people simultaneously in such a powerful way, I asked Mary, "Tell me, does this kind of experience follow your work wherever you go?"

She said, "Let me tell you a secret, Babsie. I have never seen—either in my own ministry or anyone else's ministry—what happened here tonight." She said she didn't know it could happen, never dreamed it could happen. And she said, "If you are surprised, there is no one more surprised than me. I can't believe what God has done! He must have done it here because he has some special design for the people of this nation."

What had happened was simply that under the anointing of the Spirit, these hundreds of people had all at once "rested" in the Spirit.

What Does It Mean to "Rest in the Spirit"?

Mother Angelica of Eternal Word Television Network once described this experience in this way: "It's as though the Spirit wants to work so deeply in you that he has to put you to sleep, to spiritually anesthetize you, to do his work."

Some call this experience being "slain in the Spirit," but "resting" best describes this peaceful state of "spiritual anesthesia." When it happens, the Spirit fills people in such a way that they simply fall where they are and remain in a state of deep communion with the Spirit for a period of time. This phenomenon seemed to free us, as though we had come through a stressful journey to a peaceful place. And when it happened, other gifts began to surface.

Now, it is important to realize that not everyone needs to experience this "resting in the Spirit" to receive his gifts. The Lord is all knowing, all loving, all wise and all good. The Spirit works in people's lives, when they are open to him and trust in him, according to their needs and the needs of the community and parish in which they live, work, pray and play.

I share this story so people can understand that God can and does at times perform marvelous works to convince us of his presence, power and love. There are more stories throughout these pages that demonstrate how God manifests himself to each of us and to all of us as the body of Christ on earth.

What Can I Do to Be More Open to the Spirit?

Not everyone is charismatic. Not everyone has made a cursillo or Marriage Encounter. But everyone can be open to the gifts of the Spirit. How, then, do "noncharismatics" recognize and receive the gifts of the Spirit? I say "noncharismatic" in quotes for good reason. "Charisms" means "gifts." "Charismatic" means to be gifted. All Christians are gifted through baptism. We Catholics, through confirmation, receive the fullness of the Spirit. So we are already "gifted" or "charismatic."

If Catholic people want to know more about the Holy Spirit, especially as we prepare for that great Jubilee 2000, they might consider the following. Make a novena to the Holy Spirit before the Blessed Sacrament. If a pastor so desires, he could offer such a novena to the entire parish and the Blessed Sacrament could be exposed.

People can pray individually or in groups asking God to refresh their minds and souls with the grace and gifts of the Spirit. Always, it is good to receive the sacrament of reconciliation as part of any effort of spiritual renewal—and of course to attend Mass and receive communion.

Scripture groups can reflect on how the Holy Spirit worked in the early Church and study the Vatican II documents, especially the *Dogmatic Constitution on the Church* and the *Decree on the Apostolate of the Laity.* Study these with your Bible in hand.

Parents and pastors can organize simple but meaningful ways in which to anticipate and celebrate the feast of Pentecost. The important thing to remember, as already said, is that Pentecost is not just something that happened in the past. It happens now, every day, in our own lives. The Holy Spirit is present and active in the Church.

These are just a few ideas. With a little prayer and God-inspired imagination, you will discover many other ways in which to prepare yourself to be open to the Holy Spirit. Just remember that the one essential thing is prayer and submission to God's will.

Questions for Reflection

1. Why is the Holy Spirit important to your Christian life?
2. Give one example of how the Spirit has guided the Church in the past or in the present.
3. What are some ways in which Catholics can become more familiar with the role of the Holy Spirit and more open to him?

CHAPTER FOUR

Who, Me? Gifted?

IT IS NOT EASY FOR PEOPLE TO BELIEVE God wants to give them spiritual gifts, to call them to a share in the mission of the Church, to experience the power of God here on earth. Catholics have a large case of "humilitis." Humility is good, but "humilitis" is false humility. It leads one to deny a great truth: God has chosen each one of us to do something only we can do—and he provides the grace, strength, insight, desire and ability to accomplish what he asks of us.

You see, you already have gifts and use them every day without realizing it! You have the gifts of faith and love. God has given you strength to live up to your commitments in life.

If God has given you a spouse and children, he has given you grace to be faithful and steadfast, to be loving and constant, to be compassionate and wise. The good we accomplish in our daily lives, the successes we achieve are surely the result of God's giving us his gifts.

Who can look upon a St. Francis or a Martin de Porres and not feel a deep tug and spiritual desire, "Oh, Lord, I wish I could be like that"?

Who can read the stories of the disciples in the Acts of the Apostles and not feel the desire, "If only I could have been there!" Those tugs and desires may well be God's reminder that you can indeed have spiritual gifts and you can make present today the power God manifested through those first apostles and disciples.

Wouldn't it be marvelous to be used by God to convince people that Jesus Christ is risen and is coming again?

The gifts that enable us to do what the early disciples did, and what saints have done throughout the centuries, come with baptism. They come with all the sacraments, but we need to cooperate with God to "activate" those gifts that reside in our spirits.

It became clear to us in our prayer groups and ministries that, while the Spirit had gifts for the people of God, most Catholics did not know about the gifts. Nor did they realize that they could pray for these gifts, and exercise them to build up the kingdom of God. Here I am of course speaking about the so-called "charismatic gifts," which we call the "ministerial gifts." So, even though you are not a member of any spiritual renewal movement, God has gifts for you. The Church and her Scriptures tell us it is so.

Yes, You Already Have Gifts

You already have gifts. Each one of us is born with what we may call "natural gifts" or "natural abilities." But, if they are "natural," who gave us our nature complete with its gifts? Can there be any gift that does not come from God? And if all gifts come from God, are they not rooted in God's own spiritual nature?

Let's take a look at some of the "natural" gifts. Some people are good listeners. They can sit and let others unburden themselves until they find peace through "letting it all hang out." If you have ever been burdened and had someone hear you out, you know what a gift that was for you. Perhaps you are a good listener.

We all know someone who seems to have the right answer for almost any situation. They have what we might call a "certain wisdom." They can cut through all the garbage and get to the heart of the matter and bring helpful light to any situation. This is a "natural gift" but as we will see later, it is a sign of a deeply spiritual gift that comes to us in baptism. If you have this "natural wisdom," as some may call it, it could be a sign that God has given you the spiritual gift of wisdom and is asking you to develop it through the power of the Holy Spirit. More on wisdom later.

Do you have compassion for the suffering and lonely? What a gift is such a person to the bereaved, the sick and the ignored elderly! Maybe you are a "natural born leader." Could God be calling you to receive a spiritual blessing to become involved in ministry in your parish church or in your diocese?

Some people have a strong love for the poor. Is that all "natural" or is it a gift from God, from the Spirit of God, which calls them to work for the poor, to help the poor escape the "hellish cycle of poverty"?

So, you have "natural gifts." What are they? Do you make decisions when others seem unable to do so? Have you the courage to step into a tense, uncomfortable or even dangerous situation for the sake of justice and peace among people?

You may not recognize these gifts as coming from God because they seem simply "natural" to you. However, we have to remember that God made each and every one of us. So, if we can admit we have these "natural" gifts and that they come from God, is it so hard to realize that our gracious God also has even greater gifts for us?

The Gifts Are for the Good of All

St. Paul clearly teaches: "Now in regard to spiritual gifts, brothers, I do not want you to be unaware. You know how, when you were pagans, you were constantly attracted and led away to mute idols. Therefore, I tell you that nobody speaking by the spirit of God says, 'Jesus be accursed.' And no one can say, 'Jesus is Lord,' except by the holy Spirit" (1 Cor 12:1-3).

As St. Paul tells us (vv 4-6), *"There are different kinds of spiritual gifts but the same Spirit; there are different forms of service but the same Lord; there are different workings but the same God who produces all of them in everyone."* This great apostle goes on to tell us that to *each of us* "the manifestation of the Spirit is given for some benefit." And, as we mentioned earlier, he lists the gifts that different people can receive and exercise for the common good: wisdom in discourse, power to express knowledge, faith, the gift of healing, miraculous powers, prophecy, discernment of spirits, tongues and the ability to interpret tongues.

"But," St. Paul emphasizes, "[it is] one and the same Spirit who produces all of these, distributing them individually to each person as he wishes." The Holy Spirit dispenses gifts to the people of God for the sake of the body. And we must come to the realization that God gives gifts as he discerns them to be necessary at a particular time among a particular people. He does this for his own good purpose. What could be that good purpose? That his glory and love be made manifest among men for the salvation of souls. For we know for certain that the Father's intense desire is that *all be saved!*

These gifts are available for Catholics who have not experienced spiritual renewal through one or more of the contemporary movements. They are gifts of the Spirit given to people who want to help others for the glory of God. Parents get these gifts when they try to rear their children in the ways of the Lord. I think many Catholics unconsciously have the gift of prophecy, so good are they at helping others see the truth in given situations. Others have the gift of discernment because they are so good at helping others evaluate difficult situations and complex problems.

The gifts are there for the asking. They are given as needed. One need not be called or labeled "charismatic" to receive these gifts, but one must indeed be open to the Spirit, expect the Spirit to work in his or her life, and ask the Spirit for the gifts needed to help others.

Catholics who are unfamiliar with these gifts and how to pray for them might ask their parish priests, deacons or directors of religious education to provide instruction on the gifts and even help Catholics learn how to pray for them, recognize them and be open to them.

The secret is really no secret at all! We have to be willing to let God be God and to let ourselves be used by him for his greater honor and glory and for the good of our neighbors. This is what the local parish can help us understand and embrace.

You must read the Scriptures in faith. The Bible is not just a history of what God used to do. It is a book telling us what God can and wants to do in our own lives right now. So read the Bible in faith. Ask God to help you understand and accept his great love for you and the work he has for you in building up his kingdom. No one can replace you in the kingdom. No one can do your job or give your witness. God calls *you*. He calls *me*. He calls *each of us* and *all of us*. If we are not open to the gifts and are not willing to receive them, God is deeply offended.

For example, if a wealthy grandfather offered to pay for his grandson's higher education and the grandson refused, saying that he was more comfortable working at a menial trade, the grandfather would be hurt and offended. The grandson would have disappointed his grandfather and would have deprived himself, his family and society of the fruit of that education.

Sometimes we hang on to our religion as infants cling to their pacifiers, blankets and teddy bears. Until we are willing to let go of the comfortable and let God be the Lord of our lives, we miss out on all kinds of good things. We can never be mature in faith until we have surrendered completely to God and are willing to do his work the way he wants it done.

Questions for Reflection

1. Okay, admit it. You are gifted! Name two "natural gifts" God has given you.
2. How, in your life, does the grace of God build upon your natural abilities? In other words, how can God give spiritual power to those natural gifts?
3. Ask a trusted friend or spiritual director to tell you what gifts he or she sees in your life. Ask how God has built upon those natural gifts. If your friend so desires, do the same for him or her.

CHAPTER FIVE

The Beauty of the Gifts of the Spirit

SO, YOU BELIEVE GOD GIVES GIFTS. You pray for them. And you want to accept whatever gift the Lord gives you. The gifts are given and they are irrevocable. Scripture says this. Therefore, the body of Christ should be open to gifts.

I refer again to that first night that Father Duffy came to visit our prayer group. Remember, he said that there was a beautiful gift of prayer present in our group and many other gifts as well. But if we didn't recognize them and use them, they would dry up.

It is not that God takes back his gifts. But if we don't recognize them or use them, we lose the power to use the gifts effectively. Therefore we have to remain aware of and sensitive to the gifts. We have to want them, to be "hot" after them and ask for them.

So, let's get "hot" for these gifts that God wants to give us to help others grow in their love for him.

The Gift of Prophecy

Perhaps I should warn you. I have a lot to say about prophecy. It is a gift that is sorely needed among God's people today.

It is a gift that enables people to hear God speaking to them in the here and now. As we will see, prophecy is not revelation, but it is God speaking to us.

I will treat prophecy in great length; some of the other gifts, because of time and space limitations, I will treat rather briefly, perhaps too briefly. But what you will learn about prophecy will prepare you for reflection on all the Corinthian or charismatic gifts of the Spirit. And remember, local parishes have people able to help you understand all these gifts and to grow in them.

So here goes!

When Father Duffy spoke the prophetic word over me, I at last understood with great clarity that God had really known and loved me even before I was conceived in my mother's womb. God's eyes had been upon me, as it says in Psalm 139, all through my life. He had seen my joys and my sorrows. He had cared for me in a personal way. As the Scripture says, "Before I formed you in the womb I knew you, before you were born I dedicated you, a prophet to the nations I appointed you" (Jer 1:5). I took that to heart. Before he formed you, he knew you, too. His love for you brought you into existence. His love for you keeps you alive from one moment to the next. If he did not love you, you would not exist.

In fact, Father Duffy, who had never seen me before, tapped into an incident in my life that happened when I was a young child. That incident had left a real deep wound in my spirit. Father Duffy's prophetic word brought about a long-needed healing in my heart and spirit.

When I was six years old, my father spanked me for the first time. I was so shocked because my father spanked me. I thought he loved me too much to strike me. The spanking stemmed from a lie. It was my first experience of getting in trouble for a lie someone else had said but that I had repeated. I had repeated something I heard that was untrue.

I remember my father saying to me, "I believe what you tell me, but I have to spank you because it is important that you learn that you don't repeat what other people say." It was my first experience of very strong discipline. I remember crying for months when I thought about my father spanking me. I remained so afraid of the person who had lied that my mother took me to the parish priest and asked him to pray with me because I was so frightened all the time.

Father Duffy's prophecy of the Lord saying that he had been with me and protected me all my life was an experience of healing and deliverance of all the pent-up pain and fear that I had experienced so many years before.

I will always remember Father Duffy's prophecy. I repeat it here again:

I have loved you with an everlasting love and I have chosen you that you might do a work for me. Until this day have I preserved you and delivered you again and again from lying tongues and from tigers' teeth that would destroy you.

In actual fact, over the years people have lied about me over and over again. When I heard this prophecy, I wept for joy because I now knew that God had seen what happened, that he knew what was true and what wasn't true and that he loved me then and loved me still.

I finally decided that I would never try to defend myself against lies. People will believe what they want to believe, and my defense would most often fall on ears of people whose minds were already made up. I believe that truth will find its way out of lies. So, since that time, I have tried to suffer lies in silence and rely on God's love, expressed so wonderfully in Father Duffy's prophecy, to take care of the lies.

That experience with Father Duffy put in my heart such a value for prophecy that I myself longed to prophesy. I did not know you could ask for gifts. I had been brought up a Catholic and felt as most Catholics feel—that it is proud and arrogant to tell God what you want, but rather you should just accept what you get.

But in fact, St. Paul tells us that we should seek the gifts. "Pursue love," he says, "but strive eagerly for the spiritual gifts, above all that you may prophesy" (1 Cor 14:1). When I came upon that Scripture, I felt so good that I began to ask God to give me the gift of prophecy.

God's prophetic word speaks to the heart and evokes a response. The normal thing would be that, as the word is spoken, we discern it. We know that God, in the prophetic word, wants to build us up, lift us up and cheer us up. If someone utters a word that is condemning, we know that it does not come from God and is not a true prophecy. Of course, in prophecy, the Lord can remind us of our sinfulness and call us to his forgiving love. But the truly prophetic word does not send people into despair or the pits of hell.

God can give us specific directions in prophecy. For example, after much prayer and fasting, the apostles were told to set aside Paul and Barnabas for a special work the Lord was calling them to do (Acts 13:2-3). But the principal role of prophecy is to encourage us.

I remember the first time I prophesied, it was in a dream. I dreamed that I was prophesying! When I woke up in the morning I said to the Lord, "If I can do it in my sleep, I can do it when I'm awake! And I'm asking you, please, will you enable me to do it while I am awake?" And I've had many very pleasant experiences of what prophecy can do for people.

Sometimes people are skeptical about prophecy. They ask, "Well, if it's real, how do you get it? How does it happen?" The word of God is revealed to us in several different ways. Again, as it says in Joel, when the Spirit of God comes, young men dream dreams and old men see visions. For some, prophecy comes by "word-pictures." God will speak to us in a way we can understand, to each person in a different way. As the mental picture appears, and it could be of anything, the next step is to ask God in the quiet of your heart, "What do you want to say to us?"

In my case, I usually get pictures in my mind. I will see a thing or an animal. I think about the nature of what I am seeing. Then I simply open my mouth and the words come. If you do this, if you permit God to use you to edify and build up his people, you will be surprised at the words that come from your mouth! You will be like a flute and God is playing a tune on you.

What would a chair say to you, or a bird? For example, if the word-picture is of a dove, what comes to mind is peacefulness and gentleness. God may want to say something like, "Behold, I send my Spirit upon you. Harken to his word. Open your hearts and receive from him the gifts that I want to make available to you."

Maybe a person will somehow "hear" a gurgling brook or a mighty waterfall and see in his spirit those waters rushing over rocks. The word may come, "My people, I call you to drink of the living waters that flow from my heart. Come to me, hear me. Drink freely and without price. I give you life. Be not lifeless as rocks, but live. I am the Way, the Truth and the Life."

A person has to be open to the word and cooperate with God's gift. It may mean taking a real step in faith. Sometimes, a person has simply to open his mouth and say the first word that comes—and the message begins to flow. After all, they are God's words, not our own.

It may be hard for some people to accept the fact that God gives people certain messages to build up his faithful ones. But God has said through Scripture that he has this gift and all the others for us. It takes faith to believe God and to believe in God. It takes a humble and childlike heart to be open to the gifts of the Spirit.

One very good example of the value of prophecy came in a prayer meeting many years ago. The word was, "Do not touch my anointed, for he is precious to me and I shall protect him, for he is mine."

When the word was spoken, I said to the people, "Did you hear what God said?" I was trying to stimulate people to a response to realize God was talking about them. They were anointed in baptism and in confirmation. I said to them, "You bear the sign and seal of the Holy Spirit. God is talking about you! Let us rejoice and thank him for his promise that he will defend us and protect us against the enemy."

That same morning, just as the meeting had ended, one of the girls from the community came to me and said, "Auntie Babsie, thieves entered our house. You should see the mess." I was stunned. People were waiting to see me. A rumble of unrest and shock came from them as they, too, heard the bad news. I said, "No, no. God's word to us is that we praise in times of trial. We praise. So let us praise God. Besides, God said to us today, 'Do not touch my anointed for he is precious to me and I shall defend him.' And so, I am one of the Lord's anointed and I expect that God will defend me. Therefore, not another word."

The girl asked if I were coming home. I said, "No, I will complete the work God has given me here and then I will come home." After an hour and a half of ministry, I went home. But without that prophetic word, I would not have been able to stay; I would have run home. The prophetic word had so cheered me and assured me of God's presence and providence that I was able to do what I was called to do and then go home.

When I went home, the little girl was right, I couldn't believe the mess. I thought of all the things in my house that could have been stolen. It occurred to me that I had a box of jewelry for a niece who had died and I was holding them for her little eight-year-old daughter. I thought, "Oh, dear God, if those jewels are stolen, how will I ever explain this to her father?" Again, I remembered the prophecy and I prayed, "Please God, defend me."

As I entered the house, I noticed the wrapping for the jewelry box on the floor. The box and jewels I realized had been stolen. I went into another room where I had six hundred American dollars in a box. The money belonged to Father Duffy. I felt that if the money had been stolen, I would have to find a way to repay him. But when I entered the room, the only drawer that was untouched was the drawer that the money was in. I pulled the door open and there was the money. I started to clap my hands and dance around the room.

I entered another room. The thief had obviously sat on the bed and turned out my own jewelry box. He took everything that was cheap costume jewelry and left the one genuine set of jade earrings. I was overjoyed with God's intervention in this crime.

When I returned to the first bedroom, someone said to me, "Auntie Babsie, what is in this box?" I said, "I don't know. I've never seen this box before." So she opened the box and there was my niece's jewelry. The box had been wrapped in paper and so I had never seen the actual box. The thief was on his way out with that box of jewelry when he saw a tin can with some money in it. When he found the money, he was so distracted that he forgot the box of jewelry.

God's prophetic word was fulfilled: he had indeed protected his anointed. The money in that tin was of much less value than the jewelry in the box.

I immediately took that box of jewelry, wrapped it up and dispatched it to my niece's mother! I sent her the message that it was too much responsibility for me and I hoped she would care for the valuables! Because of things like that I have come to place prime value on prophecy.

Once I was in a poor village. I looked up and saw cones growing on the electrical wires. These cones are parasitic plants, something like Spanish moss in the southern United States. I began to reflect on that plant, with no earth to nourish it. And this is the word that came to me for those people:

You are my people. If I look after the birds of the air, I will surely look after you. You are more valuable to me than many sparrows. See the cones. They draw their sustenance from the air. It is I who created them and I look after them. How much more will I look after you if you put your trust in me. I have promised you that I will meet your need. Therefore, trust me.

This prophecy really cheered people. Prophecy can at times call attention to a problem. But it always offers comfort and hope. You can see the word affect certain people. It is as though their spirit quickens. If God really speaks a word, it must quicken somebody.

Such is the goodness of this great gift. It is the *now* word. It's like a box of Kleenex. When you pull out the first tissue, another pops up. You pull that and yet another pops out. It's the same way in which the Lord puts his word on your tongue. You speak it and when the message is over, you are aware it is over.

We must be ready to speak the word that God wants spoken *now*, the word that will build up, lift up and cheer up.

Later, I will tell you about some prophecies in recent times that have great significance to us Catholics as we approach the third millennium.

Prophecy, in itself, is the Lord speaking a "now message." God always has something to say to his people. God wants to be in communication with his people. He speaks now, in the present moment. St. Paul says to us that he really wishes that everybody would prophesy. The prophet speaks to us for encouragement and solace. Prophecy lifts up, builds up and cheers up the congregation (1 Cor 14:3). Prophecy is not used to condemn.

Sometimes a person can use his own ideas to chastise the community according to his own personal insights and spirit. This is not prophecy. We have to watch out for this misuse or abuse of a great gift. The body of Christ knows when a prophecy is true or not. The Spirit of God does not abandon us or leave us orphans. When a true word comes from God, the body of Christ knows it. Discernment is given to the body as a whole or through specific individuals. The first test is that it squares with the Word of God!

Prophecy is not foretelling the future as in the case of fortune tellers and psychics. Prophecy is God's word for the moment. If a God-given prophecy does point to the future, it has its significance in the here and now.

Prophecy is "born on the tongue." In other words, it comes from God in the moment of prophecy. It is not pious inspiration received in prayer time and written out for recital at a later time. That may be good for private or group reflection, but it is not prophecy. God doesn't serve leftover dinners. When we gather together to praise and worship God, he visits with us. God will have a word to say to the people assembled there to build them up, lift them up and cheer them up. That is the word we should be looking for.

It is important to realize that prophecy is not the same as revelation. Revelation is what God gives to his Church. The Church teaches that true revelation ended with the apostles. God reveals himself to us through Scripture and the sacred Tradition of the Church. But he can inspire each Christian in a personal way. Such personal inspiration is never valid if it contradicts Scripture or the Church.

Prophecy is common after a time of praise; that is when we should listen for the word of God, because God inhabits the praise of his people. So, after he has made himself present to us in our praise, it is natural that we should expect he has something to say to us. So for a time we are quiet and we listen.

When a person senses the urge to utter a word from God, he or she may choose to do so—or choose not to do so. Prophecy is not forced upon us by God. If one has a word but does not utter it, God may be disappointed, but a person is free to choose. If we really are expectant that the Lord will speak to his people, we will offer ourselves as a channel through which he can speak to the congregation. As we listen in our hearts for God to speak his prophetic word we must remember and listen as Elijah did (1 Kgs 19:12)—for the gentle breeze. For God does not usually speak to us in the loud wind. Listen carefully for the words he speaks to you as a gentle breeze.

The Gift of Tongues and Interpretation of Tongues

Speaking in tongues is a gift in which the Holy Spirit takes over and prays for us. As it says in Romans, "The Spirit too comes to the aid of our weakness; for we do not know how to pray as we ought, but the Spirit itself intercedes with inexpressible groanings. And the one who searches hearts knows what is the intention of the Spirit, because it intercedes for the holy ones according to God's will" (8:26-27).

Here is an example of that "groaning" of the Spirit. A woman told me, "I had only one son. That son caused me more grief than anything else I can think about. He was in and out of prison. I prayed and prayed all my life for this son. It seemed the more I prayed, the more trouble he got into.

"One day," she said, "I was outside washing clothes. My mother came to tell me the police had arrested my son. I began to bawl. It seemed that my cries came out from the depths of my belly like my belly was in pain. I just doubled over and bawled and bawled. Then words began to flow out of my mouth. These strange words that sounded like nonsense just kept flowing out of my mouth.

"My mother and sister thought I was in hysteria and they got a taxicab to take me to the hospital. And still the thing kept happening. My whole body seemed to convulse and these words kept flowing out of my mouth. By the time I got to the hospital, it had stopped. The doctor gave me some medicine and I went home.

"But the strange thing is that this was the last time my son got into trouble. He never got back into trouble with the police. He got a steady job and his whole life changed. Do you think I could have spoken in tongues?"

I said to her, "I know that you did! The Holy Spirit heard the cry of your heart and presented your petition to God the Father. The Father answered the prayer of the Spirit and your son was delivered." St. Paul tells us that those who speak in tongues speak not to men but to God (1 Cor 14:2). In some translations, it says they speak "mysteries to God."

The gifts of the Holy Spirit, including the gift of tongues, are for everybody, not just for people who have made a cursillo or who belong in the charismatic renewal. When I speak to general congregations in Catholic parishes, I just explain the Scripture.

One night, I asked the people, "How many of you understand the gift of tongues or would like the gift of tongues?" Nobody put up his hand. Then I said, "How many of you would like to speak mysteries to God?" And everybody's hand went up. So, I said, "Speaking in tongues—here it is in 1 Corinthians—is speaking mysteries to God." With that realization, everybody was willing to listen. By the end of the session, everybody desired to speak mysteries to God and they recognized tongues as a genuine gift of the Holy Spirit.

St. Paul said that while speaking in tongues, in a sense, may be the least of the gifts, it is a gift for everybody, it is the gift that opens the door to a deeper and wider faith. You have to have a really simple faith in God to be able to yield to the gift of tongues, to really believe that God is at work in your soul. Many people feel like fools when they are called to the gift of tongues. They hold back and do not yield. They feel embarrassed—and the enemy really plays on their minds.

One day, not long after I received the gift of tongues, I was praying in tongues as a preliminary to prayer with the intellect. Suddenly, it was as if someone said to me, "Oh, that's idiotic! What do you think you are doing?" And I stopped for a moment, really stunned. Indeed, what did I think I was doing? It was like so much nonsense. Then I remembered and I snapped right back: "I don't care how nonsensical it is! If it's good enough for God, it's good enough for me!"

The gift of tongues opens us up to other gifts. As a gift of prayer, it is praise of God, and sometimes an entire congregation opens up to God in praise through tongues.

Tongues can also be used prophetically and for instruction. Someone may have a word from God spoken in a tongue. But, St. Paul reminds, unless there is an interpreter, no one can understand the message and it is fruitless (1 Cor 14:6-18). He says that in church, if someone is speaking in tongues, God may well be praised, but without interpretation, no one else can be edified. Tongues, then, like any other gift, is for the benefit of the community as well as for the individual.

We have to realize that the faith that gives us the gift of tongues is the same faith that gives us interpretation of tongues. We are not seeking "translation of tongues" but "interpretation of tongues." Interpretation can work in the same way that the gift of prophecy is received. As we listen to the tongues, certain impressions are formed in our hearts and minds. Sometimes, as the tongues roll, we might hear or imagine falling water. That draws up a whole pattern in our minds. Our faith tells us God may want us to give a word to his people. If we are open to the Spirit, a prophetic word from God might come forth from this image in this manner: "The living water of my Spirit continually flows to water the dry places of your life. I say to you, come all you who are thirsty. Drink without price, of the waters of my Spirit and live, for I want to refresh you."

Sometimes, as we listen, we might hear a wailing. The image that could come to one would be Rachel weeping for her children and we might hear the Lord say: "I weep, my people. I weep because you wallow in your sins instead of turning toward me to be healed. I say to you: Come to me and I will heal you. Come to me and I will deliver you from oppression. But you run away from me and you run away because of the burden of your sins, although you know that I have already paid the price for your salvation. Once again, I cry to you. Hear my weeping and return to me, my beloved ones, for I love you."

So you interpret the impression you have received from the word spoken in tongues. Also, at times, the Lord may put very deliberate things into your mind. So, when someone speaks in tongues, we ought to listen very attentively. The same God who gives the message will also give the interpretation. Tongues with interpretation equals prophecy.

The Gifts of Knowledge and Wisdom

The night my sister left the prayer meeting so ill, Father Duffy knew God had wanted to heal her. He had never seen her before and knew nothing about her, but he knew, through the gift of knowledge, that God wanted to heal her.

So the gift of knowledge is a gift of revelation about something that it would be humanly impossible for us to know by natural means. It has to be given by God. After God gives us knowledge, he gives us the wisdom to do what needs to be done with the knowledge we have. Again the Spirit reveals, as in the case of Father Duffy's first visit with us, "Come, let's pray over Babsie for her sister. The united faith in this room can bring about healing." He called us all together, laid hands on me, and then gave another instruction. "Keep in mind what we are doing. We are praying for Babsie's sister. God wants to heal her, and it will come to pass." And it did. My sister was healed in her sleep.

Father Duffy exercised the wisdom of the moment. He knew how to bring about what God had revealed to him through the gift of knowledge. The use of knowledge without wisdom may easily thwart the purposes of God and delay fulfillment. Wisdom shows us how to use the knowledge that God has given in order to help bring about his holy will for a person or situation. Wisdom tells us how to achieve something that God has revealed.

The Gift of Faith

Now this "gift of faith" mentioned by St. Paul in the ministerial gifts is not "believing faith." Believing faith is a supernatural gift from God that enables us to believe whatever God has revealed. This is the faith we receive in baptism when we receive the Holy Spirit through the prayers of the Church and the ministry of the priest or deacon. When asked by the priest or deacon what the parents are asking of the Church for their child, they answer, "Faith." This gift is believing faith.

This gift of faith mentioned in 1 Corinthians is the sudden surge of certainty, the firm conviction, the belief without doubt, that God will act in a certain situation. We find that under the power of that conviction we do things that are impossible in normal human circumstances.

I remember, for example, a nun who came to visit us with Mary Goddard. The nun had been diagnosed with terminal cancer. As they talked together, Mary prayed with her for deliverance from the disease. All of a sudden, Mary spoke to the cancer, "In the name of Jesus, I command you: Loose your hold!" The nun doubled over and vomited and was immediately healed.

How could Mary do that? Why did she do that? By the inspiration of the Holy Spirit and the surge of faith that enabled her to know without doubting that God would act. Her faith was so sure that as she commanded the cancer to leave she jerked away the tablecloth so it would not be soiled! God acted.

This surge of faith, the gift of knowledge, is seen in full power in Acts when St. Peter and St. John met the beggar at the gate. The beggar asked for money. St. Peter said, "I have neither silver nor gold, but what I do have I give you: in the name of Jesus Christ the Nazarene,... walk." Peter pulled the beggar up by the right hand and he was immediately healed. His feet and ankles grew strong and he went "walking and jumping and praising God" (Acts 3:1-8).

Most people have little problem believing that God, in New Testament times, responded quickly and miraculously to the prayers of the faithful. But many people find it hard to believe that God responds so quickly and positively to prayer in our own time. But God is God and never changes. What has changed is the faith we put in God's own promise to hear us and answer us. Also, we have to be people of prayer. The gift of faith comes with much prayer and a perpetual habit of *listening* to what God is saying. No one can expect to receive such a gift if he has not been accustomed to listening for what God has to say and then acting on it.

Deacon Henry Libersat, my coauthor, enjoys telling a faith story he heard when he was only six years old, but one he never forgot. The story was told in the 1940s but happened in the 1930s, long before modern spiritual renewal movements began. Here is his story.

My mother's friend, Mrs. Castle, had a deep faith. It was the kind of faith that said, "God is real and he hears us." She was a traditional Catholic—she went to Mass every day. Her husband was Baptist and they had two daughters who were nuns and one son who was a faithful husband and father.

Mrs. Castle had a Baptist friend who took a trip with her one day. In their old Model A Ford, they drove a dirt road under repair. Effie, Mrs. Castle's friend, had just been fitted with a new set of false teeth. They were hurting her so she took them out of her mouth, wrapped them in a handkerchief and set them in her lap.

They had a long wait on that dirt road and they finally got out of the car to stretch their legs. Effie didn't realize it at the time, but her new false teeth fell into the dirt on the road.

Finally they drove off. Some time later, Effie remembered her teeth. She said, "Oh, no! I lost my teeth. I think they are on that dirt road."

Mrs. Castle said, "Effie, let's go look. Have faith. I know you are a Baptist, but I have a friend who's good at finding lost things. His name is St. Anthony. I'll promise a novena to him and you pray, too."

They went back to the place where they had stopped the car and stood in the road. The road was a mess. Huge graders had passed over the road and dirt was piled up all over the place. Mrs. Castle said, "Have faith, Effie, and pray."

Suddenly, Mrs. Castle looked over at a large clump of dirt, walked to it and pushed it over with her foot—and there wereEffie's teeth, both the uppers and lowers, a little dirty, but completely unharmed!

So you see, the gift of faith is not new to our generation. That kind of faith has been with us since the apostolic age.

Now, I have another story for you. I remember a certain prayer meeting at which a woman took violently ill. Others went to pray with her as I continued to teach. A lady in that group voiced grave concern for the woman and suggested that I stop what I was doing and go to pray with her. I replied, "Other people are praying with her. We can continue to do what we are supposed to be doing." She said, "No, I'm very upset." So I said, "Okay, if it will make you happy I will go to pray with her."

Indeed, when I went to where this woman was, I found her alone. Nobody was praying with her. I looked around and saw someone who was supposed to be praying and I asked, "Well, why aren't you praying?" I was told the woman had asked for a doctor and they were trying to get one. I said, "This is a prayer meeting, for heaven's sake. While some are praying, someone else could be getting the doctor!"

I went over to the woman and began praying. While I was praying with her, I had a sudden feeling that she died. Sweat covered her whole body and she was as pale as death. I don't know if she really was clinically dead, but she sure looked it. I felt sure she was at least near death. Something seemed to roll up inside me and I blurted, "But you can't die. You're at a prayer meeting!"

I said to God, "Can you imagine what the newspaper will

say tomorrow? 'Woman dies at prayer meeting!' Lord, can you imagine the embarrassment of the bishop when he discovers we were holding a prayer meeting in an Anglican church and somebody died? What account can we give for this? Lord, you've got to help us! Even if she really is dead, you can help us. Lazarus was dead four days and you raised him up. So, in the name of Jesus, I speak life to this woman. Let the soul return to the body in Jesus' name!"

Immediately her face became very, very pink, and I continued to pray, "I impart life to you in Jesus' name. In Jesus' name, arise!"

She opened her eyes. I asked, "How are you?" She said, "Very weak." I told her God could fix that and I prayed, "May the power of God descend upon you and invigorate you. May the blood of Christ flow in every vein to give you life." I prayed everything that came to me. I asked, "How are you?" She said, "I feel all right." I said, "Would you like to get up?" She said, "Well, I sent for the doctor and you know how doctors are when you send for them and they come and you are sitting up...." I said, "Okay, that's all right. Lady, God bless you."

I had an assurance that God wanted to heal this woman and that I had to pray with her. That's what I call the gift of faith. A sure faith that God will act in a certain way. It may not seem at all rational, but you know that God will act. So, you act. You make yourself available for the action of God.

And the woman who insisted I go to pray with the sick woman? Well, she surely had the gift of knowledge. She didn't know why I had to go, but she knew that God wanted me to go.

The Gift of Healing

In his healing ministry, Jesus approached healing from three different levels. First, Jesus knew that a person may have a physical manifestation of illness that may not at all be based on physical deficiency of any kind. We remember that when they brought the paralytic to him and lowered the sick man through the roof (see Mk 2:1-12), Jesus immediately said to this man, "Your sins are forgiven." All sickness is the result of original sin. Jesus looked on this man and perhaps realized that his illness could also be rooted in a deep sense of personal guilt. So Jesus found it necessary to forgive his sins, and with the *forgiveness* of sin and the freedom from guilt, Jesus expected the man to walk. Jesus read the troubled thoughts of the Pharisees. So he said, "But that you may know that the Son of Man has authority to forgive sins on earth" [he said to the paralyzed man], "I say to you, rise, pick up your mat, and go home." And he did.

A second example involved *evil spirits*. Jesus saw the woman in the synagogue (Lk 13:10-13) who was all bent over because an evil spirit had drained her of strength. Jesus called to her and said, "Woman, you are set free of your infirmity." Then he laid his hand on her and she was healed. Immediately the evil spirit left and the woman straightened up.

Third, Jesus healed when there was simply a *physical illness*. Jesus encountered the leper who said to him, "If you wish, you can make me clean." And Jesus was moved with compassion. Jesus touched the man and said, "I do will it. Be made clean." The man was immediately healed and the word spread like wildfire (see Mk 1:40-45).

In the healings of Jesus, the spoken word played a very important part. When the woman with a hemorrhage touched him (Mk 5:21-34), he asked who touched him. The crowd was pressing upon him, but he knew someone had touched him with faith and for a purpose. He felt the surge of energy that left his body. He pressed on with his question until finally the woman admitted she had touched him. He spoke the word to her, "Your faith has saved you." Jesus realized that the spoken word was very important to the person being healed. So he always spoke.

Sometimes, when we receive a gift of healing, the enemy attempts to downplay it in our minds and it is easy for us to begin to doubt we have been healed. For example, in 1974 I attended the charismatic renewal conference held at the University of Notre Dame. Francis McNutt and Barbara Shlemon, two very well-known people, were ministering. They were calling out illnesses of people present and indicating in which section those people were sitting. I was astounded that such a thing was happening in a Catholic gathering.

For myself, I felt I had nothing for which I needed to be healed. I felt a deep sense of gratitude that I was well, except for the fact that I wore spectacles. I had worn spectacles for twenty-five years. My spectacles were an answer to my physical deficiency, so I didn't think it was something I needed to pray about. So I lent myself wholly and completely to praying with the healers for the people being healed. In the midst of the prayer, I was overwhelmed by the awesomeness of God and his desire to enter into our human condition and to deliver us. I began to weep. As I started to weep, I took my spectacles off and put them in my pocket. The rest of the night I just continued to pray.

When the meeting was over and I was walking down the steps of the stadium, I realized that I was seeing the steps very clearly without my spectacles. I thought, "Gee, I wonder if my eyes were healed, but I didn't ask for it." Anyway, I walked all the way down those steps with my friends. We went back to the dormitory and when we got there we wanted to do night prayer together. I took up my prayer book and realized I could see. I read all the night prayers without the spectacles and I went to bed wondering, "Could I be healed? Could I be healed? I wonder what happened? Could my eyes be better?"

The following morning I didn't put on my spectacles for morning prayer. Nobody realized that I had no spectacles. We went back to the stadium and I spent the whole day without my spectacles and I decided I would not put them back on. When I got to my daughter's home in Canada, my daughter immediately asked, "Mommie, where are your spectacles? Have your eyes been healed?"

I smiled and said, "Well, I haven't worn them in three days and maybe my eyes are healed. But I think that if I can sew without them I will accept that I have been healed."

She said, "Okay, that we can find out soon enough. I have a shirt for my husband that needs to be fixed." She gave me her husband's navy-blue shirt, and she said, "You fix that without your glasses and you will know you have been healed."

I did the whole job without spectacles—a navy-blue shirt, with navy-blue thread, without spectacles. Just in the presence of God's people praising him, I was healed even without asking.

Two days after, however, I was alone in the house and I needed to catch a plane to return home. When I took the phone book to look up the number for the taxi service, I couldn't see a thing. It was all blurred. I panicked. There were just a few moments before I had to leave to catch the plane. I had no recourse to anybody for help.

In my panic, I reached for my spectacles, but immediately I stopped and said, "No! No! I know I can see. Lord Jesus Christ, I believe that you healed me and I know I can see—but I can't see!" Then I cried out, "Jesus, I don't care if I can't see. Let your sight flow through my eyes, but don't let the devil get me." And immediately, I saw the number that I wanted and ordered the taxi.

Right away, from the tensions I had experienced, I got a splitting headache. I blurted out, "Okay, devil, do your worst. Jesus is Lord! I don't care what you do! I can see!" And that resulted in twenty years of being free from the spectacles that I had worn for twenty-five years. God had acted. If I had yielded to the panic of the moment, I would have denied the healing. I think that happens to many people. The return of any kind of symptom immediately triggers off the fear that they have not been healed. One friend of mine says, *"When God has acted, don't let the symptoms confuse you!"*

Sometimes Jesus healed just by his word. Sometimes, by touch. Sometimes, by extraordinary things such as putting spittle on the eyes of the blind man (Mk 8:22-26). Sometimes Jesus cast out demons and sometimes he forgave sins. Jesus discerned the roots of illnesses and healed those roots so the healings could be permanent. And then, he spoke the word of healing to confirm the healing.

We have learned through our experiences in the renewal that there are all kinds of healing. There are healing of memories, physical healings, spiritual healings and a healing of the soul that has been sick because of lack of spiritual nourishment from the Word of God and the Bread of Life.

To pray for healing and to help people be open to healing, to help them understand more fully their needs, their problems and God's ready power to heal them, we need to be able to discern what we see and hear.

The Gift of Discernment

Discernment is needed in every facet of our lives. It is needed by parents, teachers and employers. It is needed by preachers and confessors. Discernment is a gift to help us understand what is happening in any given situation or relationship.

We speak of discernment of spirits. That does not mean only the good spirits like angels or the bad spirits like devils. It does encompass those realities, but we also need to discern those natural "spirits," those inclinations and even hidden agendas that motivate people as they act and react in relationships and situations.

We look for the Holy Spirit himself to be in us. We start, before we can look for any other kind of discerning power, looking for his presence in our lives. How do we know he is present? Jesus said he would send the Holy Spirit. The Holy Spirit reveals Jesus. The presence of the Holy Spirit is so important to the Christian that without the Spirit we cannot say in faith, "Jesus is Lord"; no one with the Spirit in him can say "Jesus be accursed" (1 Cor 12:3).

According to St. Ignatius, the movement in our spirit can come from God—the movement of the Holy Spirit in our lives; or it can come from ourselves, a movement of our natural spirits; or, it could also come from the evil one, the movement of that evil spirit which points us away from God. One of the keys is that any spirit which admits that Jesus has come in the flesh is the Spirit of God, the Holy Spirit (1 Jn 4:1-2). When the Holy Spirit is in motion, when he is working in us, everything he says and does will glorify Jesus and proclaim Jesus as Lord.

Our natural spirits are usually more motivated by the things we might want for ourselves. The motivation comes from the desires and needs of our flesh and our natural leanings. Of course, the evil one would turn us completely away and bring us into his power. We need to pray for that gift of discernment that enables us to recognize the Spirit prompting us. It is a gift the Church truly needs today. We need, as a Church, to be able to discern when the Spirit of God is at work, when the spirit of the world is at work and when the evil spirit is infiltrating us and moving us toward things that are not of God, such as New Age-type religions. We can fall so easily and be led astray, even into idolatry, without the gift of discernment.

Discernment in Family Life

This gift is very desirable in our normal, everyday life. In dealing with our children, for example, each child is different. Each is an individual and what works for one child does not work for another.

For example, my two daughters were very similar in many ways and they were very good friends. But, I soon learned that if I promised to spank them, one would immediately recoil and do everything right because she didn't want to be spanked at any price. The other one regarded it as a threat. She objected to the threat and if you promised to spank her, she would draw you out until you finally had to spank her. So I learned that it wasn't going to be beneficial to threaten her with a spanking. I had to find another way to deal with her.

Through prayerful reflection, and the gift of discernment, I realized that if they had a party to go to, I could say to the little one that she could not go to the party unless she did such and such. She would respond right away and comply because she wanted to go to the party. The older one would do nothing; I later discovered that she hated to go to parties. Whenever I kept her back from going to a party, I would soon find her lying in bed, reading a book, having a ball all by herself. So I realized that for her, punishment should be making her go to the party. I had to deal with them on two completely different levels—and that is the result of discernment. Parents have to discern the hearts and the minds of their children so they will know how to guide them.

Another way to discern how to guide our children is to realize they have latent gifts in their minds and hearts. These are gifts from God, so we should ask God to help us recognize and affirm these gifts. We have to encourage our children to pursue and develop those gifts so they are more likely to walk in the will of God. *The Lord graces our everyday moments so we can fulfill our obligations as parents, workers, employers, teachers and friends.*

God does not leave us orphans. When he calls us to a role in life he gives us the ability to fulfill our responsibilities. I wonder sometimes whether religious people truly understand just how much God has made available to them to carry them through their lives.

God gives married couples grace. I like to think about the wedding feast in Cana. Jesus performed his first miracle there, turning water into wine so the hosts would not be embarrassed by running out of wine. I feel that when a man and woman invite Jesus to their wedding, and honor him as the chief guest, he does not come empty-handed. He comes with a gift and I like to call that gift a first-aid kit. He presents this first-aid kit to the bride and groom for their entire lives. Because he anticipates every day of their life together, he knows exactly what they will need.

This kit contains "aspirins" for the temper, and graces of patience and love and discernment so they can interpret one another's needs. There are graces of humility and trust. In that box there is everything they will ever need to live out their covenant with one another and to rear their children in the love of God.

When our friends come to a wedding shower, they give us everything they think we will need—from tablespoons to screwdrivers to sheets and towels. How much more will Jesus give us what we need?

So when troubles arise in a marriage, no matter what they are, both the husband and wife should stop together and affirm their faith that Jesus did not come empty-handed but that he gave them what they would need to solve the problem of that moment, and every moment. If they do so, God will release his grace and power into their relationship, and problems will be solved.

When couples or individuals come to me for prayer, I ask, "What grace do you think you need most right now?" I then tell them about the first-aid kit, and we pray to God so the gift can be released right then and there. Several marriages have been healed because couples had enough faith and humility to ask God for what they needed, for what he has already promised to give them to live out their commitment to one another.

All these gifts of the Holy Spirit can only be worked by the Spirit and through the Spirit. None of us has such a hold on the gifts that we can demand a certain outcome of God or tell him to work in any particular way. The gifts work only when the Spirit is active in us. We have to offer ourselves as instruments and channels through which the Spirit can work to bring about his will. Especially with the gift of healing we ought to grow daily in humility as we approach this particular gift.

Discernment in Praying for the Sick

I want to share a little story. One time a group of us was praying for a man who had cancer. We were praying that he would be healed. As time went on, some of us realized that this man would not be healed physically and that God would call him home. We thought we should be praying for him to have the grace to come to terms with God, to receive the sacrament of the sick, to be consoled, to experience the faith to face whatever would come. We felt we should pray for the grace of peace and the grace to do all that was necessary for him to put his things in order.

And there was a conflict. One woman was adamant that we should continue to pray for healing. Finally, one day, I knew that this man was going to die, and I felt it would be entirely unfair not to prepare his wife for that fact. I thought I should at least check with her to see if she knew what was happening, or we would really do her a great disservice if she were not prepared for his death.

Another person and I spoke with the wife and we discovered she also realized he was dying. So we prayed for her to have courage to go with him to the end and to be a source of courage for him. Then we went back and prayed with the man again that he should be completely relaxed in the will of God. We left. Needless to say, the lady who objected was very angry.

He died. For people of faith, we know that death is part of life and death is an open door to life everlasting, to live in the presence of God forever. As St. Paul says, we do not mourn as pagans who have no hope, but we look forward to the resurrection. (see Thes 4:13)

These ministerial gifts are given by God. We need God's help and God, as a loving Father, full of compassion, desires to equip us to minister one to the other for the sake of the whole body. The gifts and the call of God are without "repentance." God does not take back his gifts. He doesn't have to take away a gift from one person to give to another. He is unlimited and he will pour out as many gifts and as much mercy and love as are needed to heal the body of Christ. He desires that we should walk in holiness.

The gifts are not a sign of holiness—and we must be very clear about this—the gifts are a call to holiness. However, Jesus told us we shall be known by the fruits we bear as *bona fide* sons and daughters of God.

Questions for Reflection

1. Auntie Babsie spent a lot of time on the gift of prophecy. Why do you think she did so?
2. Have you ever experienced a "prophetic word" in your life— spoken by someone else or by yourself? Explain to a friend how this occurred and what it meant to you.
3. Have you ever felt a deep sense of God's presence within your heart and soul, a presence so real that you felt as though you could fly or just burst or jump for joy? What caused it? How did that experience, or lack of it, affect your way of praying?

CHAPTER SIX

The Fruit of
the Spirit

PEOPLE USE DIFFERENT KINDS OF TREES to decorate as Christmas trees. Some people have pine trees, so they use them. Others may have to use a holly branch or pear tree or a maple tree.

But, once the tree is covered with decorative lights, stockings and shiny glass ornaments, they all say one thing: "It's Christmas time!" Everyone knows a Christmas tree when they see one. But if that tree were left alone in its natural habitat to grow and bear fruit, it would not bear tinsel, lights, stockings and ornaments. A pine tree would produce pine cones; an apple tree, apples; an oak tree, acorns; a pear tree, pears—all according to the nature of the specific tree.

We are very much the same way in our Christian life. We can talk like Christians, and do what Christians do—go to church and pray and do good deeds. But we cannot bear spiritual fruit, the fruit of the Holy Spirit, unless we are converted and transformed and filled with the Spirit of God.

The Holy Spirit, alive in us, bears fruit in our lives. That one fruit is the fullness of Christian life. It is spiritual perfection through union with God. That perfection is manifested in what we normally call the *Fruit of the Spirit*.

The Catechism of the Catholic Church tells us that the fruit of the Spirit "are perfections that the Holy Spirit forms in us as the first fruits of eternal glory" (#1832).

The proof that we are really Christians, living and working in the power of the Holy Spirit, is that we bring forth the appropriate fruit. We remember that John the Baptist, when he saw the Pharisees coming to him for baptism, looked at them and called them a brood of vipers. He told them to bear the appropriate fruit of repentance. St. Paul lists nine fruits of the Spirit (Gal 5:22-23):

> "The fruit of the Spirit is love, joy, peace, patience, kindness, generosity, faithfulness, gentleness, self-control [or chastity]."

Again, note that the Scripture doesn't say "fruits" of the Spirit, but the *fruit* of the Spirit. The *fruit*—what does that mean? The fruit of the Spirit is evident in all of the nine attitudes listed by St. Paul.

The *fruit* is the manifestation of the Spirit that shows forth the attitudes of unity, love and peace. There is no love, joy and peace unless there is patience, kindness, generosity, faithfulness, gentleness and chastity. And, we can see that St. Paul combines modesty and self-control with chastity. He apparently equates gentleness with kindness.

Wherever the Spirit is at work, these attitudes and behavior are evident. Let's reflect briefly on these nine attitudes which are evidence of the abiding fruit of the Spirit. Some of these attitudes have been treated in greater length than others. This is the way the reflections came to me as we prayed over this book. You may want to meet with a friend or parish priest to better understand those attitudes of the Spirit you feel are treated too briefly here.

Love

St. Paul says that love is above all other gifts and manifestations of the fruit of the Spirit. "So faith, hope, love remain, these three; but the greatest of these is love" (1 Cor 13:13). Love is a fruit of the spirit, not a gift of the Spirit. We forget that. We get the gift of the Spirit, and the fruit of that gift, accepted and embraced in our lives, is love. "God is love, and whoever remains in love remains in God and God in him" (1 Jn 4:16b).

Love is God living in us, the result of the gift of the Spirit. *We do not love so much as we are love.* Because God is in us, we are love and our lives are shaped in love. We still must make conscious decisions in order to live and act in love. But, formed in the image of God and with God living in us, love becomes a way of life. That is part of the transformation that comes with surrender to God.

The fruit of the Spirit is guaranteed where the Spirit is at work. We should move with confidence in the fact that wherever the Spirit of the Lord is, there is love. If we are filled with the Spirit and love is lacking where we are, the Lord is making the demand of love on us and we are to put love into the situation. The Christian is not allowed to run around seeking love. The Christian *is* love and wherever the Christian is, the fruit of love is manifested.

Love is not what so many people seek to make it. Love is not lust. Love is not a good feeling, not a warm fuzzy. When someone loves, it may feel good, but it can feel bad, too. Love is doing the right thing for others as well as for yourself. What is the right thing? We have to look to the mind and heart of God.

The popes and bishops have always said that the mind of God is knowable through revelation and the teachings of the

Church. If we love one another, if we love God, we obey the commandments. The commandments are given to us to make us become fully what God calls us to be. They flow from God's love. God made us out of love. He guides us out of love.

True love is liberating. It sets us free. If we love God and one another, we do what is morally right. We do not compromise anyone's conscience, not even our own. We choose what is sometimes the hard path, the difficult road, because we want to do what is right for ourselves and for others. Jesus did not feel good on the cross, but he was doing what was right. He was obeying his Father.

Parents know how it sometimes hurts to love. To see a child go away down the wrong road, to see a loved one suffer pain and to stay there and care for that person, that is hard to do, but somehow, when we love, it becomes possible to bear the pain. Love is a power. We learn from St. Paul (1 Cor 13:4 ff) that love is kind and considerate, generous, not jealous, never rude. Love rejoices in what is right and love never fails. He goes on to tell us that we must seek after love and to do everything in love.

But what is love? "In this is love: not that we have loved God, but that he loved us and sent his Son as expiation for our sins" (1 Jn 4:10). When we finally force ourselves to face the reality of God's immense love for us, we struggle with the question, "How can I respond to such a love?" And God tells us, "Beloved, if God so loved us, we also must love one another. No one has ever seen God. Yet, if we love one another, God remains in us, and his love is brought to perfection in us. This is how we know that we remain in him and he in us, that he has given us of his Spirit" (1 Jn 4:11-13). If we do not love one another, we do not love God. "Whoever does not love a brother whom he has seen cannot love God whom he has not seen" (1 Jn 4:20b).

And if we continue reading God's Word, we learn that when we love there is no room for fear. Love drives away fear. That's why a parent can run into a burning building to save a child. That's how Jesus was able to embrace the cross, because he loves the Father and us so very much.

Love also enables us to be patient. If patience is a problem, we need only to realize how patient God is with us. We sin so often, sometimes the same sin over and over again. And God forgives us time and again, every time we say, "Oh, Lord, forgive me. I've done it again!" How can we be impatient or lack compassion for others? We are imperfect people offending a perfect God. Why can't we forgive others, especially our own imperfect children for offending us who are also imperfect? And, by the way, we must remember that it can be our own imperfections that give rise to the offending attitudes and actions in others. So, if we truly love, patience, mildness and generosity of spirit are manifest in our lives and relationships.

Peace

Similarly, the Christian does not seek peace. The Christian *is* peace. Jesus places on us the responsibility to make peace wherever we are. Our Lady continues to reaffirm, throughout all her appearances in history, that peace comes from reconciliation with God.

Peace is a fruit of the Holy Spirit that is born of a broken and contrite heart, a heart that is reconciled to God. The Christian does not simply pray for peace. The Christian *makes* peace by becoming reconciled with God and with men. The

Christian *makes* peace by exercising the option of forgiveness.

Peace is a wonderful gift from God. Peace is the opposite of anxiety. Peace is what Jesus gives us when he comes to us and when we accept him. Peace is born of love, of a relationship of love. The late Pope Paul VI, many years ago, told the United Nations that peace is not simply the absence of war. Peace is a positive power in the lives of people, families and nations. *Pope Paul VI told us that if we want peace we have to work for justice.* What is justice? Justice is giving each person what he or she truly deserves as one who possesses dignity. People have a right to sufficient food, clothing and housing. They have a right to life. The right to life is the most fundamental of rights.

No one gives us rights, not government, not employers, not even parents. Rights come to us by our nature as human beings made in the image of God. That's what Pope John Paul II teaches us in *The Splendor of Truth.* Because we are made in God's image, we have rights. Rights are built into the very nature of creation. When governments are truly interested in justice, laws protect human rights. When governments and those who govern are interested in selfish ends, then basic human rights are abused and even denied. Injustice is the result.

When justice reigns, we can see evidence of love all around us. People are doing what is right for others as well as for themselves. When justice reigns, there is peace—people have what they need because of love rather than because of political, economic or physical force.

But to bring justice through reconciliation is to live and practice repentance. Repentance follows forgiveness. If I have been selfish and have hurt others because I have not given to the poor and homeless, then confessing that sin is necessary; to repent is likewise necessary. To repent means to turn around, to change our way of thinking and of living. If I have been heartless with the poor, and if I am truly repentant, then I must begin to be generous with the poor. Otherwise, I am not truly sorry and not truly repentant.

Repentance and justice sometimes demand restitution as well. It is painful for me to do so, but I must give a personal example of how I was unjust and had to make restitution.

Father Michael and I returned home from a tour of ministry abroad. He had his old guitar with him and I had a used keyboard that, in my travels, had been given to me as a gift for the children. This gift was one for which I should have paid a duty upon returning to my own country. The customs officer was very careful. I was very tired and prone to short answers.

He asked me, "Is this instrument yours?"

"Yes," I replied.

"Did you take it out of the country with you?"

"Yes," I said, and he passed it without further question. Father Michael had answered the same questions similarly— only his answers were true!

I felt very badly in my heart, but there were other things to attend to so we pressed on. Then there was the welcoming party outside and they followed us home. It was many hours before Father Michael and I were alone again and I sensed I had it coming to me.

Without any preliminary, Father Michael said, "Why did you lie?"

I replied, "I am sorry. I feel so bad."

"You see, the sad thing is that you lied even in my presence. Pretty soon, if I'm not careful, I'll be lying, too!"

"Okay, I'm sorry," I said again.

"I hope you will go to confession before you receive Holy Communion again," he said. I told him, "I can go to confession right now if you want, but I am searching my heart to know how I can make restitution. You know, I'm sorry!"

"Well," he said gently, "I hope you can find a way," and he bent over and kissed me "good night" as though nothing had happened.

The following morning he left very early for Mass in the parish. I continued brainstorming the Holy Spirit for a way to extricate myself from my predicament. At last, it was clear what I should do. I must return to the customs office with the keyboard, admit my guilt and pay whatever fees were due.

By prayer, I received the grace to make restitution. Here I was, the seventy-two-year-old head of a charismatic community and worldwide evangelist, having to admit that I had been not only foolish but fraudulent as well. I did what I had to do that night. I sought out the chief customs officer, confessed and asked for a chance to make restitution.

It ended well, thank God! But it was such an excruciating experience that it surely brought me to a "firm purpose of amendment." I smile as I recount all this and I utter a silent prayer in gratitude to God for his unfailing love and manifold graces.

Justice comes with a price. It requires forgiveness, repentance and restitution.

Joy

Joy is not what people ordinarily call happiness. It is not being "tickled to death" by a good joke. It is not the gaiety we feel at a party. "Happiness" can be interpreted as meaning something that results from a happening, something almost accidental, something that is "lucky" or "good fortune." A person is surely happy if he or she wins the Lotto.

Joy, on the other hand, is that deep, deep sense of contentment that comes from the gift of peace. It is the result of a repentant heart or a heart whose love has at last been requited. For example, when you at last are reunited with someone very dear to you, say a parent, child or long-lost friend, you feel more than simple happiness. You feel a deep *joy*.

To be with someone who shares faith in Jesus is a source of joy. In Scripture, we read: "Although I have much to write to you, I do not intend to use paper and ink. Instead, I hope to visit you and speak face to face so that our joy may be complete" (2 Jn 1:12).

Joy is born of love and peace. Joy is knowing God and Jesus Christ whom he has sent and experiencing salvation in and through Jesus: "Although you have not seen him you love him; even though you do not see him you now yet believe in him, you rejoice with an indescribable and glorious joy, as you attain the goal of [your] faith, the salvation of your souls" (1 Pt 1:8-9).

Joy is what we experience when we at last are reconciled with God. When we come to the grace of repentance, we realize the goodness of God toward us. We realize that God has rescued us from the snares of the fowler, as the Scripture says, and rescued us from our own selfish desires. So there is nothing that can come from that experience but joy—exultant joy in the goodness of God in spite of our own carelessness about life and our own ignorance. God has made us to stand on holy ground. Our gratitude knows no bounds and joy flows from a grateful heart.

Scripture promises us:

> With joy you will draw water
>> at the fountain of salvation, and say on that day:
>
> Give thanks to the LORD, acclaim his name;
>> among the nations make known his deeds,
>> proclaim how exalted is his name.
>
> Sing praise to the LORD for his glorious achievement;
>> let this be known throughout all the earth.
>
> Shout with exultation, O city of Zion,
>> for great in your midst
>> is the Holy One of Israel!"   ISAIAH 12:3-6

Joy then is more than contagious. Sometimes little children start giggling and giggling. Their laughter seems to be contagious. Even adults experience this. If happiness and giddiness are contagious, how much more is that joy born from the love of God. True joy demands to be shared, as Isaiah commands us to "let this be known throughout all the earth."

Being in the presence of the Lord indeed brings us joy. After his resurrection and after his revelation of himself on the road to Emmaus, Jesus appeared to his disciples and they were still "incredulous for joy and ... amazed" (Lk 24:41) and after witnessing the ascension, they "returned to Jerusalem with great joy" (Lk 24:52).

My prayer for you is that you may know this great blessing of joy born of salvation and repentance.

Patience

When the Spirit is alive in us, we become aware of how patient God has been with us. As we read in the New Testament, "And consider the patience of our Lord as salvation ..."

(2 Pt 3:15). God is patient with us because he wants us to be saved.

If we are living in the Spirit, we want to be saved and we want others to be saved. Our desire to see others close to the Lord leads us to desire patience, the kind of patience which God extends to us. As we realize how patient he is with us, we are given the grace to be patient with others. There is humor in our desire for patience. We know that if we pray for patience, the Lord will give us opportunities to practice patience. As Father Duffy told us, "If you pray for patience, prepare for trial" because how else will you know if you have patience and recognize your response to trial. So we feel a bit hesitant to pray for patience.

Patience and all the manifestations of the fruit of the Spirit are graces that are inherent in the presence of God. God surrounds us and fills us. We do not run around seeking graces, but rather we are still and reach out to take those graces God so wants us to have. We must really believe deep in our hearts that where God is, so is the fruit of the Spirit; all these gifts are available to us. All we need to do is reach out in faith and accept them. This is the kind of prayer we should pray:

Lord, I know that you are here because you promised to be. In your presence there is fullness of joy, fullness of peace, fullness of life, fullness of patience and love. And anything good that we want and need is available in your presence. So, in faith, I reach out to receive, to take, to lay hold of the seed of patience that is right here, right now with me. I thank you, Lord, for infusing me with the grace of patience that makes it possible for me to wait to see the manifestation of your presence in this situation and in these persons.

So, whatever the situation, we know that in the Lord's presence we can be patient through his grace, and that in being patient many types of healing abound. We must be patient and keep faith. Sometimes, patience is hard, especially when we have something to do in God's name and something is in the way, maybe even physical illness.

I recall being at a conference at the Franciscan University of Steubenville, Ohio. The conference was on Mary, mercy and the Eucharist. I had to give a talk, but I got a drastic bout of gastric flu. I didn't think I had enough life in me to do anything at all. It was so bad that they had to send for the paramedics. They gave me ammonia, oxygen and tender loving care. It was only an hour before the talk when I was really violently sick.

All the others were trying to help. They offered to take over my talk. But I kept saying, "There is grace in this moment. God is present here and he knows why I came and that I have this to do. I expect to be filled with the grace necessary to do the talk when the time comes." With God's help I was patiently and expectantly waiting for him to enable me to do what he wanted done.

When the time came, just before my talk, they asked me if I wanted to go up on the stage. I said, still feeling miserable, "I'll stay down here and bask in the presence of the Lord, reaching for the grace of healing as long as I can. When you are really ready for me, I will come."

Finally, I went up and while I was being introduced, I kept reaching out to God to capture the grace necessary to be able to do what I had to do. I got up and virtually waddled to the lectern. But the minute I opened my mouth and said, "God is good," an infusion of grace just flooded me with the power of the Holy Spirit. An anointing fell upon me. I was able to go through the whole talk, completely, without stopping.

The people who knew how sick I was just could not believe what was happening. The people who didn't know I was sick said they saw sparks of the Holy Spirit flying everywhere. They sensed that I was surrounded by the power of God.

I can't help but feel that if we grow in a deeper consciousness that there is a whole sea of life and grace surrounding us at every moment, we will be willing simply to reach out and take what God has already held out to us. We would be empowered to do whatever we have been called to do. We will have patience born of faith and sustained in the joy of his holy presence.

Self-Control and Chastity Go Hand-in-Hand

Self-control covers a multitude of temptations and possibilities, especially where sins of the flesh are concerned—such as lust and gluttony. Self-control is essential to living the Christian life, but it can be very difficult unless we seek to live the life of the Spirit.

First, we will take a brief look at chastity and modesty. In order to be both modest and chaste, we must develop self-control through lives nurtured and refreshed in the Spirit. In recent times, modesty and chastity have fallen victim to modernism and materialism. Temptation sometimes speaks more persistently and convincingly than those who preach the gospel.

We have lost control of our youth. They know nothing about modesty and chastity because society does not foster modesty or chastity. Such virtues are scoffed at and laughed at. Now we are reaping the harvest that we sowed when we became careless about practicing these virtues and imparting them to our children.

A friend of mine explains it this way:
Society, in too many parts of the world, has embraced an attitude of immediate self-gratification. People have lost the sense of sin and they don't realize that God, in the beginning, made us perfect and we are truly happy and filled with joy only when we are fully in his will. Jesus is the Way, the Truth and the Life. The Commandments were given to help us become fully human, to show us the way to be fully capable of being one with God.

When people are interested only in self-gratification and when they believe the world revolves around them, there are no truths or principles greater than their own little selfish and childish desires. This is so obvious when it comes to "sins of the flesh" such as adultery, homosexual relations and fornication. People deny the commandment because it gets in their way. Their own personal feelings and passions are more powerful than their mind and spirit. They silence the call of conscience and shut out God for the sake of personal "fulfillment," which is nothing more than personal destruction!

Chastity is a fruit of the Holy Spirit that is not reserved for priests and those who have taken vows of celibacy. Chastity is for all the people of God. Chastity means using one's sexuality according to the mind of God. Only married couples may engage in sexual relations, which must always be open to new life. Premarital sexual relations, adultery and homosexual relations are sinful.

Modesty says that our bodies are sacred, but today people expose their bodies without shame. I really feel that pornography, swarming as it is all over the world, is fostered and encouraged by the fact that we have rejected the fruit of modesty and chastity. And the prevalence of pornography makes it difficult to convince people that it is wrong and both spiritually and socially dangerous. It is spiritually dangerous because it leads us away from God. This, of course, is socially dangerous, but add to that the phenomenal increase in instances of violence motivated by rampant sexual desire!

When I speak of *self-control*, I am also reminded of the importance of controlling my temper. If I can boast of any weakness that is especially my own—one which I inherited from my father—it is the "gift" of anger. My father had a temper that was so volatile!

At age fourteen, I discovered I, too, had a temper. It happened one morning when I was late for school. My brother, who is four years older than I am, was sitting in a chair that blocked my way to the sewing machine. I asked him to move and he didn't. He pretended not to hear me. He just ignored me completely and kept on doing what he was doing.

Now, in my mother's house and in our culture, you never hit anyone. Especially you never hit an older person. But when my brother ignored me, I just flipped and I fell upon him like a thousand dragons! I hit him all over.

He was twice my size. He got up and all he tried to do was defend himself. He never hit me back. But I was screaming and crying at the top of my voice. My mother heard me and she thought I was the one being attacked. She came running inside and when she saw what was happening, she was appalled. She kept calling my name, "Babsie! Stop it! How could you do this to your brother? Stop it!" And her pleas did not reach me.

She did the most amazing thing. She just turned round about and disappeared for a minute. She came back with a machete. She said to me, "If you want to kill him, you will do it with this a lot more easily and more quickly." The shock of it brought me to my senses. I just broke down and wept and wept uncontrollably.

Needless to say, I missed school that morning. I just couldn't go. I was out of it. My mother didn't say another word, but the reality that I was capable of murder hit me like a ton of bricks. After I got over the shock, I promised myself that I would never get angry again. And I kept that promise. For years and years after that I would laugh at most things. People would say, "You let people take advantage of you. Do you never get vexed?" And I would respond, "When I get vexed, I'm not pretty. I pray that you will never see me vexed."

However, years later, I did get vexed. My boss got me so angry I stormed out of his office, picked up my typewriter and screamed, "I'll throw this damned thing right through that window." But, somehow, I found myself putting the typewriter back on the desk and I ran to the restroom where I cried for a long time. I realized I had succumbed again to a wild anger. Finally I went back out to my desk and no one said a word. It was very, very quiet. When all the others were leaving for home, I was staying late to catch up on the work I had not done while in the restroom. One of my friends, one who always said I let people take advantage of me, came to me. She leaned over my shoulder and whispered, "Never get vexed again!"

But I did get vexed one more time. Years later, I was so angry with a woman in our community that I felt I could have killed her. I had an errand to do in the city. On my way,

I realized I was so seething with rage that I had not prayed for a parking place. In our city, parking is a real problem and I usually prayed. So, as I entered town, I told God that I was in no way deserving of a parking place, that I was so full of anger and resentment that I had no merits on which I could rely for his consideration. I told him that if he provided a parking place I would be grateful and if he did not I would certainly understand.

As I approached the building where I was to do business, a man backed out and left me a large parking space right in front of the door I had to enter. As though that were not enough, the woman I needed to see came out the door, saw me and came over to the car! I finished my business with her and sat there in my car crying. "What kind of God are you?" I asked him. "Not only the best parking space possible, but you bring out this lady to meet me at the car!"

I decided then and there I had to do something with this temper once and for all. I went home and began to pray. I decided to speak to the woman with whom I was so angry. I called her and she came. When I explained my anger, instead of saying, "I'm sorry," she began to defend herself. I experienced the anger rising again. I said to her, "Listen, I called you to make peace, but right now this tiger is rising in my tank. Get out or I'll kill you!" She literally propelled herself out of that room.

When I was alone again in the presence of God I said, "God, I don't believe this. Can you imagine the papers tomorrow morning, 'Head of community kills member'? Can you imagine the archbishop's embarrassment when he picks up the Trinidad paper? Lord, you've really got to help me. Why couldn't I treat her the way you treated me? What is wrong with me? Help me,

God." Once again, I doubled up and began to bawl. God spoke to me in my heart. I realized he was saying to me, "You lack compassion. Pray for compassion."

When that woman did wrong, my response was "She's no good. She should be out of here." Instead, I should have been thinking, "Poor thing. In spite of all the privileges she's had, in spite of all the gospel she's heard and all she knows, she's still in this condition. Poor thing, what can I do to help her?" That would be the compassionate thing to do.

Compassion means "to suffer with." And I surely had suffered with her. I know what it means to fail, to repent, to be forgiven and to be reconciled. The grateful thing to do would be to extend to her what God had extended to me—patience unto salvation.

Calm and peace came over me, and from that day I have prayed for compassion and for the grace to respond to circumstances the way Jesus would respond to them. So, the Lord helps me to control this tiger that is always there, never dead, only asleep, waiting for the right stimulation to rise up again.

Anger, of course, is one of the seven capital, or deadly, sins. (The others are pride, lust, gluttony, envy, avarice, and sloth or laziness. They will be discussed in a later chapter.)

The grace of God helps us to do what St. Paul counsels, "Be angry but do not sin; do not let the sun set on your anger, and do not leave room for the devil" (Eph 4:26-27). The emotions that we have are God-given. They are part of our lives. But they can either bring us to death or actually give us power for life on the level of the Spirit.

Anger generates a lot of energy in us. Anger could empower us to rescue a child—or even a pet—from grave danger. At one time, I raised rabbits. I loved those little rabbits. I used to set them on the table and feed them watercress from my plate. One day a dog snatched one of my little rabbits. I was filled with fear for my rabbit and that fear created a deep anger.

I fought that dog to rescue my rabbit. The rabbit was dead when I forced the dog to drop it, but I was not about to let that dog eat my rabbit.

Anger gives us a lot of power and we can use it either constructively or destructively. If we have self-control, the anger can be controlled and we can use it constructively.

It isn't too difficult to see how the fruit of the Spirit, those beautiful graces, help us to overcome our "structural weaknesses." Later, when we reflect a little on the Isaian gifts of the Spirit—fear of the Lord, piety, fortitude, counsel, knowledge, understanding and wisdom—we will see how those gifts also heal and strengthen us to overcome these "structural weaknesses."

Patient Endurance

There is patience, and then there is patient endurance. One can be *patient* with an obnoxious person met only occasionally. But it takes *endurance* to live with such a person day in and day out!

This great fruit of the Spirit is also evidence of God's presence in our lives. If we gently accept all that befalls us as the persistent plan of God for our eternal good, we can greatly profit from our earthly trials. Everything depends on the way we take things and patient endurance allows us to see how the crosses of this world can have supernatural merit now and in the life to come.

Nothing God gives us or allows to happen to us is without the expressed purpose of drawing us, and even others, to his loving arms. He persistently prods us closer and closer to him.

Little trials draw us to him. Driving in Trinidad is actually an exercise in patient endurance. These days everyone thinks that the road is his own. Cars block passage; some drivers wind in and out of traffic, causing others to slam on their brakes and shake their heads. Some use their horns more than their brakes! Each one thinks his own mission or errand or meeting is the most important thing going on in the country. But everything depends on the way we take things!

With the gift of patient endurance, we can surmise that the Lord is allowing that car to nearly run into ours because the driver needs our prayers and the Lord is bringing our attention to the driver so that we can pray for him. The Lord may want us to be stuck in that traffic jam so that the group in the car behind us may see and ponder our bumper sticker—"Jesus is Lord!"

Great and heroic trials can show forth this fruit. St. Ambrose spoke of the patient endurance of David. He said that when David was insulted by Shimei with hateful curses and stoning, David held his peace and humbled himself. David patiently endured the hatred and pain to grow in humility before the Lord God (see 2 Sm 16:5-14).

With patient endurance, we bear wrongs willingly for we see that a great good can come from the way we take things. We can better follow the Lord's command to turn the other cheek. We can take up our cross and follow him. We can pray for our enemies and do good for those who hurt us. We can in all things give thanks to God.

Wrapped in each unpleasant experience is a jewel of infinite value. His most precious gifts sometimes appear to us to be wrapped in dirty newsprint.

Kindness

This fruit disposes us to treat people as though they were really our brothers and sisters—and they are! It helps us to be considerate of others, to care about them and their needs. It helps to take us out of ourselves and to see others' virtues and needs. It helps us to love them even when in a worldly view they are surely hard to love.

Oftentimes, when we pray for those who are very hard to love—when we accept the Spirit's prompting to kindness—not only do we begin to love these unlovable folks, they actually *become* lovable to us! So the fruit, when accepted and used, produces many other fruits. It changes the "kind" person to a loving one and pours blessings on the object of the kindness. Kindness blossoms into compassion and softens our world-hardened hearts. It gives us a bit of the Lord's sight so that we start to see others through his eyes.

Generosity

Generosity places proper ownership on our assets—whether they are worldly riches or spiritual ones. Generosity shows us that God is the owner of all good things and convicts us of our responsibility to be good stewards of his riches.

Generosity enables us to give to others with ease. It detaches us from our worldly goods and lets us see these things as tools for Jesus' use. It gives us giving hearts and releases us from ties to the world.

While kindness recognizes a need, generosity works to fill that need. While kindness disposes us to see others as our brothers and sisters, generosity prompts us to share the family inheritance—and more than that. Well exercised, this fruit will compel us to give all and then, with empty hands, to ask the Lord for more.

Generosity prompts us to spend our lives in others' service. Mother Teresa is the most visible beneficiary of this fruit in our time. Not so long ago, the world experienced Maximilian Kolbe's generous gift of his life. This priest, now recognized as a saint in the Church, was a prisoner in a Nazi concentration camp in World War II. A prisoner escaped, and the Nazis decided to execute, by starvation, ten prisoners in his place. One of the ten chosen was a married man with a family.

Father Kolbe volunteered to die in the place of this man, announcing to the Nazi commander, "I am a priest." He and the other nine were placed in a starvation bunker. There they all starved to death, except Father Kolbe who, the Germans found, was still alive after several days. So they injected acid into his veins to finish him.

What greater show of generosity than Father Kolbe's courageous act? None. As our Lord told us, there is no greater love than the love that will lead us to lay down our lives for another (Jn 15:13).

Faith

Faith, as a manifestation of the Spirit, improves our supernatural vision and hearing. The hand of God becomes readily apparent in events of life. We can more clearly see not only the "signs and wonders" of our times, but we can see God's work and love in our own everyday lives.

For example, when the Berlin Wall came down it was to many of us a great sign of the power of prayer. We had prayed for so long. And, in our own daily lives, we see God helping us love when it is difficult to love. We see him answering prayer for employment, health and healing.

As this gift of faith develops, we begin to speak with the Lord throughout the day about our needs—for a parking place, for a break in traffic, for a visit from a favorite friend. Then we see God's loving hand in fulfilling those needs!

We begin to understand St. Francis. Once when sitting on a little hill and enjoying the pasture flowers, he stood up, looked to heaven and told the Lord: "Lord, I know you are with me. You don't have to shout." The beauty of that little pasture's flowers screamed of God's presence to the dear saint.

Once, a priest observed a simple little man sitting for hours and hours before the exposed Holy Eucharist. The priest became curious and asked the man what he was praying about. The simple little man said, "Nothing. I just look at Jesus and he looks at me." He saw Jesus so clearly he would look at him as he would look at the person he loved most in the world. Two lovers exchanging affections by looking into each others' eyes. Such faith! Such keen vision!

Meekness (or Mildness)

Meekness is a great manifestation of the Spirit. In it we see Jesus' Sacred Heart, and that of his Holy Mother.

An old prayer says: "Jesus, meek and humble of heart, make my heart like yours." This fruit shows his heart in action. We become St. Francis' prayer in action and it becomes "second nature" for us to see the meekness and humility of God in his incarnation, his life, his ministries, his Church's sacraments—especially the Eucharist.

We want to be instruments of God, his servants, his empty

vessels, his tools to be used as he wants to use us. Like St. Theresa, we want to be toys of the Child Jesus—ready for him to pick us up and use us for his pleasure.

We come to think little of the world and see more clearly that this life means little except as it is used in God's service. We become servants to God and to those he places in our lives, and we enjoy and revel in that servitude! We see our whole beings in a new perspective and want to be "used up" in God's service until "It is no longer I who live but Christ who lives in me," as St. Paul said.

Questions for Reflection

1. Have you ever met someone with whom you immediately felt you could be a good and lasting friend? What gave you that impression?

2. In what ways does the Holy Spirit manifest his presence in your family? In your parents, children, spouse or good friend?

3. In your quiet time, ask the Holy Spirit to enter into your life in a new and more powerful way. Ask him to bear fruit in your life, fruit that will last.

CHAPTER SEVEN

Seven Magnificent, Transforming Gifts

"IT IS THROUGH THE GRACE of the sacrament of confirmation," we used to say, "that we receive the Holy Spirit in order to make us strong and perfect Christians and soldiers of Jesus Christ." As I became aware that there was no manifestation of the Spirit's power in my life, that definition kept going around in my mind.

Since I had been confirmed, why did I not have the power to be a strong and perfect Christian? In fact, I realized I didn't have the will to be perfect. Generally speaking, people believe that perfection is impossible. Yet, the Lord Jesus tells us, "So be perfect, just as your heavenly Father is perfect" (Mt 5:48). As practicing Catholics, we so often scoff at the idea of perfection. It seems that many people today regard perfection as a vice rather than a virtue.

I had received the spiritual gift of baptism in the Holy Spirit, or as we say, the "release of the Spirit." In the charismatic renewal, the ministry gifts mentioned in 1 Corinthians were strongly emphasized. We have already discussed these.

When I realized that every Christian was given the power by the Holy Spirit to minister these gifts in their everyday circumstances I really felt cheated, since I had never been taught in the

Church to acknowledge and use these gifts. I had never heard of these gifts being exercised except at the great shrines—for example, at Lourdes and Fatima. I began to wonder why the Church did not call lay people to embrace fully those ministerial gifts.

It was about that time that I discovered in the prophet Isaiah (11:2-3) those transforming gifts poured into the hearts and souls of all Christians:

> *The spirit of the LORD shall rest upon him:*
> *a spirit of wisdom and of understanding,*
> *A spirit of counsel and of strength,*
> *a spirit of knowledge and of fear of the LORD,*
> *and his delight shall be the fear of the LORD* ....

I began to realize that these transforming gifts, the gifts that change us from ordinary human beings into sons and daughters of God, were foundational and a prerequisite to exercising the ministry gifts properly.

As someone once said, "You have to be a Christian before you can do what a Christian is supposed to do." It is in this context that we discover the truth about the statement that *faith is a gift*, freely given by God.

It is those wonderful Isaian gifts that transform us, that make us manifestly Christian, that sanctify us, make us holy and enable us to surrender to God and become his instruments of peace, healing and forgiveness.

In confirmation we received the Holy Spirit in his fullness. We received a package deal of seven sanctifying gifts: wisdom, understanding, counsel, knowledge, fortitude, piety and the fear of the Lord. I realized I had never received any instruction on what those gifts really were and what they were to do in my life. We knew the names, but not the content and value of the gifts. I began to search out their meaning and what they did for us.

My Search for Wisdom

As a child in Trinidad, after receiving confirmation, I was given a little prayer book called *Key of Heaven*. Every child had one of those books as a confirmation gift. In this little book was a prayer for wisdom, to be recited after Communion. We prayed it every day after we went to Communion. I prayed it continually and with intent. I wondered what wisdom was, but never asked anyone.

In the years of my intense search for God, I began to realize that many people understood wisdom as the knowledge you acquire from living and what you learn from the books you study. It was seen as the knowledge you amassed as you walked through your life, learning from others, from books and from life experiences. So wisdom for us lost its spiritual dimension and got mixed up somehow with mere acquisition of worldly knowledge.

I began to grapple, in the debris of my limited understanding, to see what, in all the worldly wisdom I had acquired, was there that would endure to this day and to life everlasting? It was amazing that in this time of my life, the people I found myself talking to were Protestants. In our cosmopolitan situation, I found people of every faith and persuasion. I spoke to Adventists, evangelicals, pentecostals and others.

Every time I talked to them, they gave me a quote from Scripture. I began to feel that a knowledge of Scripture was lacking in my life. I had a good neighbor who was an Adventist.

We would talk at night when I had a question or sometimes we would just talk over the fence. We would look at the Bible together. But always, our conversations were about scriptural things.

It was this person, through our relationship, who helped me begin to discover spiritual wisdom. It came about one day when she told me, in a very nice way, that I did not keep the Sabbath properly. We were talking about a bazaar we had held at our school on a Sunday. She said, "You Catholics have no respect for the Sabbath." I took issue with her. She pointed out the things that happened at the bazaar—a lot of drinking and rowdiness and gambling. So I didn't argue further, because I realized she was saying some very interesting things.

As a result of that conversation, I began to reflect on the definition we had of the Sabbath in our catechism. "You are bound to keep the Sabbath holy by attending Mass and resting from servile work." Immediately, I was able to see that for a lot of us, if we did go to Mass, we were pushing for the Mass to be finished within an hour. We were adamant that the priest not preach too long. I realized that many times, during the Mass and especially during the sermon, I would be thinking about all the things I had to go home to do.

It became clear to me that I was not really observing the Sabbath but maybe only going through the motions. This was a sign of the beginning of spiritual wisdom. I was beginning to see things through eyes of faith rather than through spiritual routines that, for me, had no real personal depth. I became more aware of the evangelicals who criticized us for not living the gospel but of bending it to suit our own individual needs. No one with a sensitive conscience could escape that indictment.

With this new insight, the transforming gifts—or the sanctifying gifts—of the Spirit suddenly took on more value and special meaning in my life. It's amazing how much wealth you can have and never explore it. To a large extent, this is what happens to most of us. God instills in us these seven, beautiful gifts to make us spiritually wealthy—but we never open the gift packages. We just admire the wrappings. So, I began to think of these seven sanctifying gifts—wisdom, understanding, knowledge, counsel, fortitude, piety and fear of the Lord—as *guaranteed* to us to *make us a holy people.*

Some Wisdom About Gifts and Giving

Through the many and varied experiences of my life, I developed a very critical attitude towards "gifts." For me, gifts are spontaneous gestures prompted by personal values such as love, gratitude, admiration, and similar movements of the heart. I remember how one of the young men at high school often placed a red rose on my desk, but I never caught him at it. So, for a long time, I didn't even know who the admirer was!

As an adult, I have been disturbed by the number of "gifts" that are given under extreme pressure, especially at Christmas and other festive times, that leave the donors overburdened by debt or embarrassment. One simple person in my life who taught me the "secret" of effective gift-giving was a paternal aunt who was never married. Her life was one of genteel poverty, but she had the beautifully unique gift of "gift-giving."

Aunt Milly always turned up with exactly the thing you needed—which made you jump around and clap your hands rejoicing even though it cost very little. I recall especially the time she brought me a dozen clothespins that cost eight cents! On a previous visit she observed I was using straight pins to keep my clothes on the line. I made innumerable mental notes to buy clothespins but always forgot until the next wash, when I just improvised again! I learned from Aunt Milly that the greatest gift was not the one that cost the most money, but rather the one reflecting the donor's love and concern for you personally. She just knew how to "gift" her friends every time, sometimes just by turning up at the right moment and giving herself.

In my life in the Spirit, I developed real hang-ups about people straining themselves to give gifts out of a feeling of obligation and I did all I could to discourage it. One day, a really poor member of our community brought me a large, heavy gift-wrapped box as a Christmas gift. I felt she was violating all my teachings on the subject, but I restrained myself and just politely accepted it, wondering what on earth could be so heavy and where could she have got the money to make the purchase. Really irritated, I put it on a shelf and forgot all about it.

Several months later, she came to visit one morning and spent about two hours with me while I was preparing lunch in hope that she could share some before leaving, but the beans just would not get soft. As she got up to say goodbye, I apologized profusely that I could not offer her lunch because of my predicament with the beans.

She looked at me quizzically and asked, "Auntie Babsie, what did you do with the pressure cooker I gave you at Christmas?"

My mind virtually exploded, as I exclaimed to myself, "Pressure cooker? Oh, God! I don't believe this! That gift-wrapped box on the shelf is a pressure cooker!" I then blurted out loud, "Girl, I have been so busy, I haven't had time to read the instructions, and I hear pressure cookers can be dangerous if not properly used."

She said, "Auntie Babsie, go and bring it." Sheepishly, I went to the shelf and, taking the box down, quickly tore off the wrappings and returned to the kitchen with the gleaming new gift in my hand. My friend set to work and eight minutes later we were sharing a delicious meal.

The more I reflect on that experience, the more deeply I conclude that *many of us Catholics, because of false humility, fail to accept and use the wonderful gift of the Holy Spirit given in the sacraments of baptism and confirmation.* The Holy Spirit is the power of God given to us from on high to enable us to meet the tough challenges in our daily life and to profit thereby. He is indeed our spiritual Pressure Cooker, who saves us invaluable time and energy and releases the joy of fellowship with God and our fellow men.

Our God is the most generous gift-giver. He gifts us because he loves us and wants to provide for all our needs, both material and spiritual. Let's make sure we don't leave them unopened.

Exploring the Gifts

It is essential to spiritual health and growth that we explore these beautiful, transforming gifts of the Holy Spirit. I recall the accuracy of the words of Dr. Josephine Massyngbaerde-Ford of Notre Dame University—"the gifts divide but the fruit of the Spirit unites."

Many people in our renewal movement had been powerfully blessed with many of the Corinthian ministerial gifts, but dissensions had arisen. There were jealousies, wrangling, arguments, pride. There was the tendency to believe that certain gifts gave us a higher position in the community. We were actually living in contradiction to the words of Jesus that leaders had to become the servants of all. There was no foundational understanding about what sanctifies us and enables us to exercise gifts safely in the will of God.

So we had to learn what the Church says we must receive to be transformed into the image of Christ. I began to realize the depths of the wisdom of the Church. It was as if she said, "Only holy people can exercise power gifts without destroying themselves."

Through this realization, I developed a real joy in the Church, a tremendous joy in the fact that the Church so desired to make us into a holy and contemplative people. It became absolutely important that we understand the sanctifying gifts. In this quest, I came upon Dr. Joseph Bajiakas who gave me a copy of his little book, *Mighty in the Spirit*. To my great delight, this little book was all about the sanctifying gifts. It explained how these transforming and sanctifying gifts were manifested in the lives of people who had been renewed in the Spirit.

If we are indeed to refresh our lives in the Holy Spirit, we will want to reflect more deeply on these gifts.

Wisdom

In the Epistle of James (1:5-8) we are told to pray for wisdom. "But if any of you lacks wisdom, he should ask God who gives to all generously and ungrudgingly, and he will be given it. But he should ask in faith, not doubting, for the one who doubts is like a wave of the sea that is driven and tossed about by the wind. For that person must not suppose that he will receive anything from the Lord, since he is a man of two minds, unstable in all his ways."

I had prayed for the gift of wisdom since I was seven years

old, at the time of my confirmation, right through to that day, and I found I had no wisdom. So, I began consciously to pray for wisdom, still not understanding what it was.

One day, I was at work helping a patient prepare for her examination by the doctor. She was relating to me all her different problems. As we talked, I tried to point out to her certain things about her concerns. At the end of the conversation, when she was ready for the doctor, I said to her, "Okay. God bless you." And she said to me, "Thank you, Mrs. Bleasdell, for all the wisdom you have shared."

I said, "Wisdom? I don't know that I gave you any wisdom. In fact, I'm always praying for wisdom but I am not sure that I have any." She said, "I would have you know that in the last twenty minutes when you spoke to me, all I heard was wisdom."

I left the room laughing, but perplexed. As I got outside the room, I said to the Lord, "Jesus, I've prayed so much for wisdom and I don't know that I have it. But she said that all she heard was wisdom."

Immediately, in my spirit, I heard the Lord come right back: "Wisdom? *I am Wisdom!* Wisdom is not something that you acquire and carry around on your back in a knapsack. No, I am the source of all wisdom, and when you are in me and I am in you, I release it to you moment by moment as you need it. I give you my wisdom so you may be able to deal with things wisely."

Still, someone may understand wisdom to be a gift for ministry rather than one for spiritual transformation. The Isaian gifts are about transformation. The key is the Lord's condition for wisdom—"when you are in me, and I am in you."

It is here that one acquires wisdom, the kind that transforms us into the image of Christ. When we are one with God, then it is easier for us to surrender to him, to put his mind, his thought, his will ahead of our own. It is easier for us to try to make our own minds into the image of God's mind, to see his way, his truth and his life far superior to our own. In fact, when we are in God and he is in us, we can say with St. Paul, "... yet I live, no longer I, but Christ lives in me; insofar as I now live in the flesh, I live by faith in the Son of God who has loved me and given himself up for me" (Gal 2:20).

When Christ lives in us, through the power of the Holy Spirit, we are transformed into his image. That is the ultimate reality of wisdom. It is not a thing, as I have said, but it is the very nature of total and complete conversion—and that kind of conversion enables us to live as God would have us live. That is wisdom. We know we are living in wisdom when we shun the vain pleasures of the world and seek the eternal treasures of God.

Knowledge

This gift refers not to scientific knowledge or even theological knowledge. It is not the information we have stored up in our brains. This gift is knowledge of God and knowledge of self. Again, it is not knowledge *about* God or about oneself. This gift implies a deep spiritual intimacy. It builds and solidifies our relationship with God.

Through the gift of knowledge, we come to know God personally. We can embrace him as Trinity, and embrace him with great joy, without understanding Trinity. We simply know him and love him for what he is, as he is and because he is.

Because we know God intimately, we can look at ourselves honestly. We can see all our faults and wounds through God's eyes. We can come to love ourselves and to forgive ourselves because we know God so well that we know he loves us even when we have not been as faithful as we should. In fact, this spiritual knowledge of God leads us to a new and purer experience of sorrow for sin. We become sorry for the gross ingratitude we have shown to God who has loved and given us so much. This kind of repentance finds its source in our knowledge of God's goodness, that intimate knowledge which draws us to him ever more closely and helps us desire holiness ever more fervently.

Older Catholics can reflect on this in light of the catechism we studied so long ago. We were taught that "God made us to know him, to love him and to serve him in this life and to be happy with him forever in the next." To know him, to really know him, is to love him. To love him is to serve him.

It is by the Holy Spirit that we come to know God. It is the Spirit who gives us this gift of knowledge through baptism and strengthens it in confirmation. It is the Spirit who leads us and guides us as we use this transforming gift as the power and the fuel to move us toward an ever deeper relationship with God.

Fortitude (Strength)

I had always understood that the power of the Holy Spirit gave us the ability to be brave in crises and to meet the challenges of our lives and to persevere in good works. In spite of whatever we encounter—ingratitude, slander, whatever—we are able to carry on, to press on, because of the power of the Holy Spirit working in us.

Also, with the Spirit, we can do extraordinary things. Throughout salvation history, believers have needed extraordinary strength to face and endure persecutions. In the Old

Testament, for example, two stories stand out immediately. Eleazar, a prominent scribe among the Jews, chose death rather than break God's law. His tormentors promised him prestige and wealth, even asked him to pretend to eat pork in order to spare his own life.

But Eleazar refused, "in a noble manner, worthy of his years," and he met his death. Under the blows and the scourging, Eleazar said, "The LORD in his holy knowledge knows full well that, although I could have escaped death, I am not only enduring terrible pain in my body from this scourging, but also suffering it with joy in my soul because of my devotion to him" (2 Mac 6:18-31).

As we read further in this holy book of the Bible (7:1 ff), we read about the widow and her seven sons. They suffered unspeakable tortures because they would not deny God and break his law. This poor widowed mother was forced to watch each of her seven sons tortured and executed before she bravely met her own death.

Such stories of heroism continued into the Christian faith. St. Paul himself, as Saul of Tarsus and before his own remarkable conversion, persecuted the Church and arrested Christians. He watched as they were stoned to death. In fact, he served as an official witness and concurred in the stoning of our first martyr, St. Stephen, one of the first seven deacons (Acts 7:1–8:1).

John the Baptist was beheaded because a lecherous man was manipulated by a wicked woman. All the apostles suffered martyrdom except for John the Evangelist. We know from history how the Roman Empire continued to persecute Christians and killed them in their arenas and by crucifixion and fire. The blood of martyrs is surely the seed of the faith, and the Tiber River ran red with that blood.

Even today, Christians of all faiths suffer martyrdom. We

read of the deaths of missionaries, of bishops, priests and sisters killed in their own native lands because they dared to live and preach the gospel. Even Catholic lay people suffer torture and death. And in countries where violence is less bloody, lay people sometimes suffer for their faith in their places of employment. They are continually passed over for raises and promotions.

But fortitude is not only about courage in the face of persecution and danger. Fortitude is a gift that many Catholics need in everyday life, but they never ask for it. Fortitude is the gift that will help Catholics overcome their timidity when it comes to sharing and defending their faith. Fortitude is a gift given us in baptism. But so many of us never surrender to that gift, never ask God to make it come alive in us. Fortitude is nourished by a gift of extraordinary faith and brightened by the gift of hope and empowered by the gift of love.

We all need to be courageous today. In a world so filled with violence, where nothing is sacred, not even the lives of born and unborn children, Christians need to be strong and courageous. We must speak out for goodness and kindness and against oppression of the mind, body and spirit of people whose lives are being crushed under the heel of misused and abused power.

Piety

The gift that really surprised me was the gift of piety. I had always assumed that the gift of piety meant that you were pious in your response to the grace of God, pious in your attitude. It blew my mind when I discovered the real meaning of piety. I learned that piety is not just "spiritual etiquette"!

Piety is the gift of sonship. The Holy Spirit gives us the grace to cry out, "Abba! Father!" We really come to know God as Father and understand ourselves as children of God, heirs of the kingdom and joint heirs with Christ. That filled me with exultant glee, to come to realize that all the treasures of the kingdom were ours as God's adopted sons and daughters. If we really believe, and it is only by the power of the Holy Spirit that we *can* really believe, we can see this clearly, what it means to be heirs of the kingdom.

We are pious because we are heirs of the kingdom. Piety is not the external manifestation of proper disposition in prayer. It *is* proper disposition in prayer. It is not externally expressed reverence for God. It *is* reverence for God. It is not believing in our sonship through Christ. It *is* our sonship in Christ.

Now, *if we have proper disposition in prayer and reverence for God in our heart of hearts and embrace our sonship in God won for us by Christ, we will manifest that piety through acts of love and devotion.* We will act as sons and daughters of God are supposed to act. Prayer will be a great blessing rather than a chore. Our neighbors will be images of God and brothers and sisters in Christ rather than people whose hands we limply shake at the greeting of peace at Mass. Our lives will take on eternal dimensions as we realize the kingdom is *already* ours, right now, in and through Jesus.

This gift can be a key that unlocks a vast treasure chest, the treasure chest of all the Spirit's ministerial gifts. If we truly believe we are coheirs of the kingdom with Christ, if we truly believe the kingdom is ours, we will more readily stretch forth our hands to say, "Here I am, Lord. I have come to do your will. Give me the gift of prophecy. Give me the gift of healing. I am your son, your daughter, Lord, and I want to show the world how much you love. Give me the gifts I need to bring others to you, their Father, their Savior and their Comforter."

Fear of the Lord

Fear of the Lord is deep reverence for God and for his Word. It is the kind of reverence that Scripture describes in a man who *trembles* at God's word. It is the kind of reverence that enables us to respect the laws of God, not just acknowledge that God and his laws exist.

Fear of the Lord goes hand in hand with knowledge and love of the Lord. How can we come face to face with a God who has no beginning and no end—who needs nothing and no one, but still creates out of love—and not feel such a deep reverence and awe?

God is awesome, in the truest meaning of that word. When we encounter God, we can only stand in awe. "Awe" means the ability to inspire dread and the mingling of dread, veneration and wonder. Awesome is a word used too loosely today.

We might say, "This celebrity is awesome." But he isn't, is he? He doesn't inspire dread. He may inspire false veneration and wonder—but he has no power in himself to inspire them. He cannot make anything at all from nothing. Every note he plays, every lyric he sings, every line he recites is all done with gifts given him by God. Likewise, we cannot call *awesome* that new video game or the latest action movie.

But God is indeed *awesome!* He always was, is now and always will be. He alone is unchanging. One God, mighty God, awesome God, holy God, Triune God. He made all things from nothing. He willed the universe to be and it was. He willed us to be and we are. Now, that is *awesome*—and I stand in wonder before my mighty God. I stand in awe. I stand with fear and trembling before such a power that could simply will me out of existence. And I stand in veneration and in love for he has chosen to make me, to give me not only life, but his Spirit as well. He has chosen to let me know him, to love him and to serve him. He has called me to eternal happiness.

Yes, before that God I stand in fear, in dread, in veneration, in wonder and in love. Yes, that is truly a gift. Fear of the Lord gives birth to piety. It is the foundation of all the other gifts, the beginning of all the other gifts. For example, as we stand in *awe* of God, we can see that the gift of piety is not merely spiritual etiquette, but the spiritual guts, blood, bone and sinew of God's relationship with us as his adopted sons and daughters. That is the truly awesome gift we call piety, and it finds its roots in the mystery of God's awesomeness and our total dependence on him. If we stand in awe before God, and in right relationship with him, the Scripture comes to life in a new and real way: "The beginning of wisdom is the fear of the LORD..." (Prv 9:10). Wisdom is at work in you when you have that kind of respect for God.

With the gift of the fear of the Lord, you will not court danger because of your respect and reverence for God, his will and his Word.

Counsel

People often decide they need someone else's advice or guidance. We consult friends and sometimes we feel the need for an attorney for legal matters. And in spiritual matters, we have many counseling structures set up in the Church.

It is good and right that we have people who can give us advice and guidance. Qualified people can help us discern what should be done. However, generally speaking, many people do not understand that within them is a "built-in Counselor," the Holy Spirit.

I remember that in the past, when I had a serious decision to make, I would discuss it with every friend and with all kinds of people and had trouble coming to a decision. At last, when I couldn't wait anymore, I simply did what seemed best—and then continued to worry about whether I had done the right thing.

It was worry, worry, worry. I worried about what I had to do. I worried about whether I should do it and how to do it. I worried about getting advice and then whose advice was best. I made up my mind and then continued to worry about whether I had been right in my decision. Only when I could see results would I lose that sense of anxiety. If I discovered I had done the wrong thing, I would mentally flog myself.

After the release of the Holy Spirit in my life, I discovered the gift of counsel was active in me. Cardinal Mercier's prayer, after all, asked the Holy Spirit to enlighten, guide and console me.

I came to realize that when the Holy Spirit enlightens you, you look at things completely differently: not through the eyes of the world or flesh, but with the eyes of faith. Through the eyes of faith, we look not for immediate benefits, but in the light of long-term effects and benefits.

And sometimes, when you are truly enlightened by the Holy Spirit, you may find the need to be consoled; you may like what you see. Or you may need strength to carry out what you learn through the Spirit.

I'll give you a story. A woman once came to me and said her son had returned home from Venezuela. He had been there several years. He came back with a young woman who he claimed was his wife, and said that he had been married in Venezuela. His mother believed him and they moved in with her. Also in her home was her sixteen-year-old daughter.

Now she had this other young woman in the house, who was only about eighteen or twenty years of age and who was allegedly her son's wife. They all lived together. She told me that she didn't know why, but she began to become very anxious about this young man and woman. She told me, "I feel as though something is wrong, but I don't know what." So, I said to her, "Why don't you pray the prayer to the Holy Spirit? Pray carefully. Pray deliberately and from your heart. Ask the Holy Spirit to enlighten you."

I prayed with her and gave her a copy of Cardinal Mercier's prayer and she went home. A few days later she came back, very agitated. She took me by the hand and said, "Come, I must talk to you. This morning I saw the girl crying. I asked her why she was crying. She told me that she believed she was pregnant. She said that she wasn't married at all to my son, that they were just together and living with me unmarried.

"Auntie Babsie," this poor woman said, "I feel as though I am going mad. If my husband learns we have this unmarried pregnant girl in our house—with our unmarried, young daughter—he'll blame me. He'll say, 'You stupid fool, why didn't you know this?' I'm frightened and I don't know what to do."

Her husband was a harsh man. He would have blamed everything on his wife and would not have seen it his responsibility to help his son find a solution to his problem. Some men, even today, have such an attitude. They do not really take responsibility for their household. They become head of the house and they find everything is wrong but they rarely give you any practical help.

So, this poor woman realized she could not keep this unmarried, pregnant girl under her roof. She began to cry. I said,

"Remember what you prayed. You prayed for enlightenment and you have been enlightened. You need to pray for consolation. 'Console me, Holy Spirit! Console me!' And then, 'Holy Spirit, tell me what to do. Guide me.'"

So we prayed together the entire prayer and stopped in reverence when we came to that part of the prayer that expressed her need for consolation and for guidance. We prayed for her son and his girlfriend, who had deceived her and put her in a difficult situation with her husband and violated the sanctity of her home. We prayed and she went away.

A week after, she came back beaming. She said she went to the parish priest and she told him about her problem. He told her that they could make arrangements for the young couple to get married very quickly and quietly without letting her husband or anyone know about the problem. She took that course and everything was resolved. The woman and her husband had sufficient resources to help the young couple set themselves up in their own home. The baby was born in wedlock and no one ever knew when the marriage took place.

In that situation and in that time and place, a quick marriage was judged a solution. People realized that marriage was for life, "until death do us part." People understood the permanence of marriage and the Church's teaching about marriage.

Of course, today this woman's problem would not be resolved in quite that fashion. Given conditions in the world and the contemporary need for more preparation for marriage, the Church does not let people rush into marriage just to solve an embarrassing problem. Attitudes today are different, and the Church has to help people—who are conditioned by the world to see marriage as a mere convenience or social custom—to understand the nature of Christian marriage.

For myself and my discovery of the gift of counsel, as I continued to pray to the Holy Spirit, I began to realize that I was making decisions without realizing I was making decisions. I was able to do the things I had to do, even very important things, without anxiety and with great peace. The gift of counsel had begun to work in my life.

Something else became very clear. Ever since I was very young, people would come to me and tell me their troubles. I would try to help them find a solution and give them little prayers to say. I always asked myself, especially when I was a young woman, why was it that people burdened me with their troubles. I never realized that God knows the gifts he has given us, and he sends his people to those he has gifted to receive from us what he has entrusted to us for their sakes.

So, this is another way in which the gift of counsel works. On the one hand, the Holy Spirit gifts us with his counsel for our own problems. On the other, he gives the gift of counsel to a person for the sake of others. It is the Holy Spirit who enables us to think of the right word of comfort when we speak with a person whose heart is torn with grief or whose spirit is buried in fear or resentment. It is the Holy Spirit who calls to our mind the right Scripture when we open our mouths to advise others.

And more, still! Just as he deals with us here on earth, by giving gifts to us and directing other people to us to receive the benefit of these gifts, he directs us to the saints who are in heaven. We go to St. Anthony if we have lost something, to St. Cecilia for concerns about music, to St. Jude when situations seem impossible and so on. The Spirit never sends us on a futile search. When he directs us, we are sure we can find the help we need.

And that is indeed *refreshing!*

Understanding

The gift of understanding is the power to understand mystery. We are able to understand spiritually things that we could never capture in our minds—such as the gifts and ways of God. It takes an illumined faith to embrace the great mystery of God's love for us, the mystery of the Trinity, the Eucharist and the communion of saints.

As we have heard for many years, the gift of understanding enables us to accept the fact that God loves us as much as he loves Jesus. He wants to treat us as he treats Jesus. Through Jesus we have become God's adopted sons and daughters. We are coheirs, with Jesus, of the kingdom of God.

These are not mere words that we speak in shallow sentimentality. They are words that speak the eternal truth of God. They are true words of hope! People are spiritually impoverished until they *understand* in their hearts what it means to be a child of God, to inherit the kingdom, to be loved by God as he loves Jesus.

We must pray to the Holy Spirit to give us this great gift. We can *understand* that we have been forgiven and are now transformed by the Spirit into the very image of Jesus. To *understand* that great mystery is to become a new creation. It is to *believe* what we say we believe. Spiritual understanding is like conviction. Our belief is unshakable because we, as some people say, "know that we know that we know" that God loves us and makes us his own.

Saying that we "know that we know that we know" is just a way of saying we are firmly convinced, that our faith is unshakable, that we are so enlightened by the grace of the Spirit that no argument, no challenge can dislodge the belief that God is in us and we are in him and that everything he has is ours.

These are the seven gifts given us by the Spirit. They are ours, by yielding to God. It is by the grace of humility that we come to keep these gifts, to realize they are gifts that we receive freely. Humility enables us to accept these transforming gifts without exalting ourselves over anyone else. We recognize the goodness of God, the love God has for the Church and the Church for God. We come to recognize God's purpose for the Church through the ages and the ultimate triumph that God has prepared for us, his Church.

We are destined to be a holy people of God, a royal priesthood, a holy nation of people set apart for the praise and the glory of God. We must desire what God desires for us. We do not merit it. We humbly accept it.

That's all part of what it means to refresh our lives in the Holy Spirit.

Questions for Reflection

1. How did this discussion of the transforming gifts of the Holy Spirit affect you? Did you learn something new? If so, what? Discuss your thoughts with a friend.

2. Choose one area of your life for which you need wisdom. Pray every day this week for the Spirit to give you wisdom in this situation. What happened? Share with a friend.

3. Which of the transforming gifts do you need increased in your life? Ask the Spirit to fill you with that gift in a special way this week.

CHAPTER EIGHT

Dangers the Spirit
Helps Us Overcome

The Power of Repentance

As WE MOVE TO REFRESH OUR LIVES IN THE HOLY SPIRIT, we must be completely realistic. The Holy Spirit does impart his gifts to us. We want to be open to them and to receive them so we can grow in holiness and in the service of our Lord. But we must never fool ourselves.

There is one who does not want us to know, to love and to serve God. He is our enemy. He works to destroy us, to discourage us, to divert us from the path to holiness. Satan is his name.

The devil is real. Don't let anyone tell you he is not real. He throws temptations in our way to make us stumble and fall. He tries to entice us away from God. He wants us to embrace the seven deadly sins instead of the seven transforming gifts of the Spirit.

Because of the effects of original sin, our human nature is weakened. We are prone to sin. The enemy works on those weaknesses. *The Catechism of the Catholic Church* lists seven capital sins: pride, avarice, envy, wrath, lust, gluttony and sloth. Let's look at each of these to better understand how the devil tempts us. With that understanding, we will be even more motivated to beg the Holy Spirit to transform us from day to day by his seven transforming gifts.

Pride is at the heart of all sin. When a person is proud, he puts himself at the center of everything. It is his way, his happiness, his pleasure. Pride has different degrees and stages, but it can lead ultimately to the hatred of God. It turns its back on God. It even, at its worst stages, curses God because it sees God as the one who tells us not to sin and who punishes sin. It is the greatest sin, the worst danger; the "original sin." Pray fervently for *humility!* Beg the Holy Spirit to transform you with his gift of fear of the Lord.

Avarice and *envy* are sewn from the same passion for personal gain. Avarice is the inordinate desire to keep what one has, not to want to share it with anyone. Avarice is what fuels the amassing of wealth while others go without the essentials for life with dignity. It is extreme selfishness.

Envy is the desire to have what belongs to another. It is okay to desire, for example, another man's property and it is okay to obtain it by legal means, by buying it, receiving it as a gift or inheriting it. However, envy would justify in a person's mind any means of acquiring what one desires. We can look to David and his lust for Bathsheba. He even went as far as murder to get another man's wife. Pray fervently for the virtue of *charity!* And ask the Holy Spirit to increase in your life the transforming gift of piety.

It is easy to see how avarice and envy stem from pride. You know, it is really difficult sometimes to separate these sins one from the other. They seem to go hand in glove. One makes room for the other. One leads to the other.

Wrath is that kind of anger that leads to violence against self or another. It is rooted in envy. Cain was envious of Abel because Abel's gift to God was more fitting. His envy led to wrath, to the desire to wipe off the face of the earth that which caused him displeasure. However, wrath is sinful long before it leads to murder. Wrath can lead to all forms of violence—lying about another person and destroying a good reputation, spreading gossip, slapping or hitting another.

No matter how good we are or how hard we try, the danger to sin is always present. We can never let down our guard. The Scriptures remind us: "Be sober and vigilant. Your opponent the devil is prowling like a lion looking for [someone] to devour" (1 Pt 5:8). Pray for *meekness of heart* and to *bear wrongs patiently!*

Lust, gluttony and *sloth (laziness)* are what we call "sins of the flesh." They are directly related to appetites of the flesh, but they are never to be seen as divorced from the spirit. These sins, too, are rooted in pride because they are concerned only with personal pleasure regardless of the cost to oneself or others.

Lust, the Catechism tells us, is "disordered desire for or inordinate enjoyment of sexual pleasure. Sexual pleasure is morally disordered when sought for itself, isolated from its procreative and unitive purposes" (#2351).

In the world today, lust is mistaken for love. People who are engaged often feel they have a right to sexual intercourse. And there are those who believe sex is nothing more than recreation and they engage in it without any thought of commitment or love. Still, they call this "making love." Love cannot be "made" in this way. It is not love. Even for engaged couples, sexual intimacy is not true love. True love desires what is best for the beloved. Sin is not what is best for oneself or for another.

The *Catechism* tells us that those who are engaged to be married are called by God to live in chastity (#2350). They are to abstain from sexual intercourse. Engagement is a holy time, a time for mutual respect and patience, a time to see deeply into a relationship to discover the inner beauty of the beloved. Abstinence for a loving couple is a time to learn fidelity—fidelity to the other, fidelity to God, fidelity to oneself and one's faith. Chastity requires true love. Lust is rooted in selfishness and pride.

The sins against chastity are many: producing, promoting or using pornography; masturbation; fornication; and adultery. Jesus said that looking on a man or woman with lust in one's heart is the same as adultery (see Mt 5:27-28). Because it is contrary to God's life-giving sacrament of marriage, homosexual activity can in no way be a holy expression of love. Pray for a *pure, chaste heart!* And ask the Holy Spirit to give you the gifts of knowledge and understanding.

Gluttony is an inordinate desire for food, and an inordinate pleasure in eating. There is the old saying which people laugh about: "Some people eat to live, but I live to eat." It's funny when we say it, but gluttony is not really funny.

Overeating is not good for one's health. It is a selfish habit, an abuse of God's great gift of food. It is wonderful to enjoy a good meal and sweets. It is another thing to overeat simply because one enjoys the taste of food.

Gluttony hurts others. We have probably all seen a child quickly wolf down candy or cake before it can be shared with others. We have all seen how some people cannot wait in line to get their meals but rush ahead of everyone else. Eating food is not a private matter. It is a social celebration.

Even when we eat alone, we are engaged in an act that celebrates all of life, that celebrates the benevolence and providence of God. To eat is to admit dependence on God for life itself. By eating with reason and in a spirit of gratitude, we acknowledge God's goodness. That is why we say grace before and after meals: it is a good way to keep one's perspective about food and nourishment.

When a person eats more than is needed, that person is eating what belongs to someone else. Pope Paul VI said that when we have too much and hoard our possessions—and I see this as including food—then we are holding on to what belongs to somebody else. God is provident. He has given the world enough food for everybody. But the "haves" do not share with the "have-nots." Pray for *temperance*!

Sloth (or acedia) is a spiritual laziness born of presumption. We fail to pray fervently because we have come to believe we have it made with God. We grow lax in prayer life. This is a terrible danger to one's soul. It can even cause us to refuse the joy of knowing and loving God. We become so self-satisfied and complacent that we think God is happy to be at our service and to wait patiently for us to take notice of him. It is true that God is patient with us, but we can never presume on that patience and the love he has for us. To presume we are really "in" with God no matter what we do or do not do, is to fool ourselves terribly and confuse truth with untruth.

A Christian must always be vigilant when it comes to prayer, confession of sin, repentance, fasting and good works. We can never take God for granted. Indeed the devil is a roaring lion waiting to jump upon us from the shadows of spiritual indifference to devour us in an instant.

Of course, there is physical laziness as well. To refuse to work, or to work in a sloppy or haphazard manner that is less than one can achieve, is sinful. It is born of pride and self-centeredness. Laziness refuses to see the good that one's work can do for others. It can be an injustice to a parent or an employer, a friend or a coworker. Physical laziness is a sign of spiritual laziness.

St. Paul tells us that he who does not work should not eat, and that people should earn the food they eat by working quietly (2 Thes 3:10-12). And Pope John Paul II has frequently spoken of the dignity of work. Work is one way in which we participate in God's work of creation. When we work, we exercise that creative kernel placed in us by God. Work cannot be seen only as the curse Adam incurred for his sin. No, it is so much more. Work is hard and sometimes unpleasant because of sin, but when one works in a spirit of surrender to God and as a way of serving God and others, then work becomes a joy rather than a burden, a prayer rather than a curse. Work is a reflection of the creative nature of God.

Surely, if one is spiritually alive and in tune with God, there will be good fruit in one's entire life—in prayer, work, play and in all relationships a person has with God and with others. In fact, we read in the Epistle of James: "Demonstrate your faith to me without works, and I will demonstate my faith to you from my works." (Jas 2:18b) Pray for a *holy zeal!*

These capital sins—pride, avarice, envy (jealousy), wrath, lust, gluttony and sloth—are always ready to rear their ugly heads. It is the Holy Spirit who gives us the power to crush these root sins, if we want to crush them.

Presumption Is Also Pride

Presumption is one danger we face after the Spirit has illuminated us. Presumption is the danger of our exalting ourselves, thinking that we are so much better than we are, that we have made ourselves holy through our own efforts and good deeds. Pride can take over and everything God has done can so easily be ruined. In presumption, we begin to mistake our will for God's will.

For example, people misunderstand one verse in Scripture and get themselves into all kinds of trouble: "If you ask anything of me in my name, I will do it" (see Jn 14:14). Based on this, people ask all kinds of things, even things that are contrary to the Scriptures and the will of God.

One night, a young woman came to me after a prayer meeting and asked me to pray with her. She was a divorcée with four children. She told me that the next day she was "setting up house" with a certain man who I knew had himself been divorced two or three times. "I want you to pray that things will go well for us," she said.

I said, "I can't pray for that." She said, "Why? Didn't God say, 'Ask anything in the name of Jesus and you will receive it'?"

So I said, "Yes, but God also said to ask him according to his will and God has specifically spoken on this. First, you are a divorcée. This man is a divorcé many times over. If you do what you are planning to do, you will be committing adultery and God has specifically said adultery is forbidden. It is a sin. No adulterer will enter the kingdom of God. We cannot go to God and pray for something that is against his will."

She said, "Okay, well, what can you pray for? Pray for anything you can pray for."

So I said, "I can pray for wisdom for you to make the right decision." She agreed and so I prayed for her to have the gift of wisdom. In fact, I asked the Holy Spirit to stir up in her all of his sanctifying gifts so she would know the right thing to do. But, of course, as you can well imagine, she continued with her plans. She never intended to cooperate with God's grace in this situation. She resisted it.

Sin Has a Long Tail

That woman lived with this man and pretty soon afterward, she became pregnant. The child was beautiful, but quite mentally disturbed. When the little girl was fourteen the mother brought her for prayer. I remember thinking, "This sin has a fourteen-year-old tail, and God alone knows how much longer it can get."

Now, God didn't punish this child for the mother's sin. No, but we do know that the mother's sin had some effect on her child.

Let me give an example. We had a cherry tree in our yard. Every year, as some of the fruit fell to the ground, many little cherry trees sprouted up. They grew for a while but soon died because they were under the big tree and could not get enough sunlight.

When children grow up under the shadow of their parents' sins, they, too, are denied the spiritual light that God sends to them through their parents. Who knows what healing and forming power this parental light has? Who knows whether this is the real cause of the child's behavioral problems? But we know one thing for sure, an unrepented sin has a long tail. The mother was distraught, tormented by the sickness of her child, tormented by what she herself had done. She knew she had done wrong and somehow blamed herself for her child's disease.

Parental sin can and does overshadow the children so that the light of Christ cannot break through. You do influence your children. You bring them up in the light of your own understanding or in the shadow of your ignorance. For as long as the shadow lasts, the children remain under the power of sin. Presumption casts a long shadow.

So, when we speak of praying in the name of Jesus, we do not ask for our own will. We pray in the nature and the Spirit of Jesus. The more we acquire the nature and spirit of Jesus, the more authority is given to us so that we ourselves can do what Jesus did. And Jesus never did anything without consulting his Father. To do so would be to offend his Father. Jesus was without sin. The perfect nature of the Father was in him. So, in his own human nature, he knew that he had to be in submission to the divine nature which he also possessed. That's what Jesus wants to teach us, that when we pray in his name, we pray in his nature, in his way of obedience to the Father's will in all things.

The Power of Repentance

When we have caused pain to the body of Christ through sin, we realize that we have done wrong. We may wonder how we can extricate ourselves from this situation and how we can repair the damage that has been done.

This is the time we embrace the beautiful gift of repentance. Through the grace of a good conscience, we become aware that our behavior and choices have had bad effects on those around us and on the Church itself. With that awareness, the only response that God accepts is that we assume responsibility for our sins. The only genuine cry that we can make from the depths of our hearts is, "Oh God, be merciful to me, a sinner."

The night before Jesus died for all our sins, he looked down the corridors of time and he saw the enormity of the task the Father had placed on him. The burden of sin that he bore to the cross included my sins and your sins.

We have a tendency to blame everybody else for the wrong decisions that we make. In order to bring light into our own lives and light into the lives of those who are affected by us, we must admit our sin and seek God's mercy. We must have no excuse but stand before God and ask his pardon. King David gives us a beautiful example of repentance in Psalm 51 (vv. 3-4):

> Have mercy on me, O God, in your goodness;
>> in the greatness of your compassion wipe out my offense.
> Thoroughly wash me from my guilt
>> and of my sin cleanse me.

But David goes on, helping us to realize that repentance is not mere regret and sorrow that we have sinned. Repentance means to turn away from sin and back to God. David sings (vv. 12-14):

> A clean heart create for me, O God,
>> and a steadfast spirit renew within me....
> Give me back the joy of your salvation,
>> and a willing spirit sustain in me.

Still, David tells us by his example, there is even more for the truly repentant spirit to do (v. 15):

> I will teach transgressors your ways,
> and sinners shall return to you.

True repentance embraces all of these movements of one's soul: (1) sorrow for sin because of the offense it has been to God and the harm it has done to others; (2) a change in the direction of one's life as we move from self-centeredness to looking for the good of others, from selfishness to generosity; and (3) we help others to see that sin is deadly and that God forgives, heals and gives us everlasting life.

To recognize our sin and how it afflicted Jesus is to feel great sorrow for offending God and hurting others. It is only in this realization that we can experience true repentance and seek the forgiveness of God. God has said to us that he will hear our cry, he will forgive us and deal with the effects that our sin has had on other people. Day by day, as we continue to cry out, God will do for us exactly what he did for David. David was a murderer. But he repented. And God referred to him as a man "after my own heart." God will say that we are after his own heart once we repent and respond to the call to be utterly humble before God.

Part of the evidence of humility is confession of sin. We must admit our sin to God. For Catholics, the sacrament of reconciliation is a great gift that enables us to experience and celebrate both forgiveness of sin and reconciliation with God and the Church. Whenever the Virgin Mary has appeared to help us grow closer to Jesus, she has urged confession of sin, repentance and special sacrifices to show God how sorry we are for having offended him.

Another evidence of true humility is compassion. When we are humble enough to admit our own sins, we are not as quick to judge others. We are better able to forgive others—our parents, spouses, children, siblings, coworkers, employers, and neighbors. We will even be able to forgive our enemies.

Repentance is really a gift of God. God does not expect us to live with perpetual guilt and constant recrimination. He expects us to come to him with our burden of sin, and from the depths of our hearts to ask for forgiveness. The power of the Precious Blood washes and cleans us. From then on, our whole lives become a blessing and we become channesl of grace, of wisdom, of love and life to the whole world. We are sustained in that holy condition by the grace and power of the Holy Spirit as we continually invoke him. The fruit of repentance is joy and gratitude.

As we recognize God's goodness and mercy, as we increase in holiness, our joy in him overflows and touches others. In a real way, our peace and joy, given and sustained by the Holy Spirit, call others from darkness into light. As Pope Paul VI said in his encyclical, *On the Evangelization of Peoples,* the best way to evangelize is to live a holy life.

I am so grateful for the following prayer from the Salesiman Missions. I pray it frequently each day, especially when I encounter sin in others or am confronted by my own sinfulness.

Special Act of Sorrow

Forgive me my sins, O Lord, forgive me my sins; the sins of my youth, the sins of my age, the sins of my soul, the sins of my body; my idle sins, my serious voluntary sins, the sins I know, the sins I have concealed so long, and which are now hidden from my memory.

I am truly sorry for every sin, mortal and venial, for all the sins of my childhood up to the present hour. I know my sins have wounded Thy tender Heart, O my Savior, let me be freed from the bonds of evil through the most bitter passion of my Redeemer.

O my Jesus, forget and forgive what I have been. Amen.

Questions for Reflection

1. What are the three movements of the repentant soul?

2. Although Auntie Babsie did not have time or space to do this, see if you can match the seven gifts of the Spirit against the seven deadly sins. How does the pursuit of God's holiness hold evil at bay?

3. What can you use from this discussion on sin and forgiveness to help a friend who is spiritually struggling?

CHAPTER NINE

The Power of Forgiveness

WHEN WE HAVE SINNED, we pray and long for God's forgiveness. He forgives time and again, for such is his great love for us. The Holy Spirit fills the Church with the power to absolve us from our sins, with the power to forgive one another. Jesus tells us we must forgive one another. If we live under the influence of the Holy Spirit, we want to forgive. But sometimes it is hard to understand how to forgive, or what it means to forgive.

Forgiveness means this: that, from our own perspective, we restore our relationship with the offending persons to the way they were before we were offended. That is what God does when he forgives. He forgets the sin. It is a new beginning. It is as though the offense never happened. That is what it means to forgive.

That is very difficult. I used to say that I would forgive but I could not forget. How can you forget? Yet, the word of the Lord is to forgive and to *forget because he forgives and forgets*. This ability to forgive is a gift. We cannot do it on our own accord or by our own strength. The Holy Spirit gives this power to us. Part of our being refreshed in the Holy Spirit is to renew our commitment to forgive, to relearn, maybe, how to forgive.

I recall a day when Father Michael, who lives in our community, and I had a very serious impasse. He said something that immediately wounded me, and he immediately apologized. He tried to make up right away, saying that what he had said was not true, that he was only being rash. But it was a real censure on my character and attitude. I told him, "No, no. Not so easy as that. I need to internalize what you said. If there is truth in it I must repent." I told him I did forgive him but insisted that I had to internalize what he said.

He went to bed without saying good night as he would normally do, and without asking for a blessing. But about midnight, I heard him coming back down the stairs. I felt glad that he was coming back, because this would have been the very first night in our continuous relationship over ten years that we would have gone to bed without making peace.

As an older person, and as one to whom he looked as a mother, I should have been the one to initiate reconciliation, but I didn't and couldn't because I really wanted to be sure that what he said had no truth in it. I told him again that I forgave him, but I wanted to think about what he said.

The next morning, on his way to say Mass in the parish church, he came to me as usual for his blessing. As he approached me, it came to me that this young man was much too good to be kept waiting for reconciliation. Immediately I said to him, "Father Michael, you are much too good, much too sincere, much too faithful and much too loving for me to let the devil come between us." He bent over and kissed me and I blessed him and I forgot completely what the issue was. This is God's miracle!

That is the kind of forgiveness that God wants to enable us to give, the kind in which we not only forgive but we forget. God says to us, "When I forgive, I forget. I remove your sins from you as far as east is from the west. Nevermore will I remember your sin" (based on Psalm 103:11-12). That is the kind of heart he wants us to acquire in our daily relationships one with another, in the Church, in the family and wherever we are.

A Tough Call to Forgive

There was another experience in forgiveness that was hard, but it was the work of God in my life. As I've already said, I had been separated from my first husband. This ended in divorce, as did my second, ill-advised marriage.

I had been apart from my first husband for about twenty years. I had enough to be resentful about, and I was resentful, but thanks be to God, I had been able to put aside many things. Some of them were just swallowed up in the sea of time.

One evening, I got a telephone call from a relative who asked me where my husband was. I said, "Whom do you mean? My Lord Jesus Christ?" He said no and he called my first husband by name.

I told him I had no husband but the Lord and I did not know where that former husband was. Wherever he was, I said, he could stay there. The caller said, "He is in Trinidad and he wants to see you."

I replied, "Then tell him that anything we have to talk about, anything that we have in common, they are more than twenty-one years old and he can talk to them." I was referring to my children.

The young man pleaded with me, "But he needs you,

Babsie. He really needs to talk to you. Will you please say yes?"

I said I would have to pray a lot about that. I prayed all night long. Finally, I agreed that I would see my former husband. When I went to see him, I saw a man ravaged by five strokes, with very impaired vision. He asked me without any pretense at all, "Babsie, have you come to take me home?"

"Home? Impossible!" was the response ringing in my heart. But he was as needy as a child about five years old. All he wanted to do was to go home. He needed to talk, to have some time with me. I went off for a moment to pray and to talk to a younger friend of mine who didn't even know I had ever been married. I told her I needed to have God's answer. Since he was remarried she said I couldn't take him home. It could cause a scandal. "I know," I told her, "what it means humanly speaking, but I want to know what God thinks."

So, we knelt down at the side of a bed. I have never seen anyone approach God more directly than this young woman did that day. She began to pray in the Spirit. She stopped and asked, "Is there anyone at home who could answer you if you made a telephone call?" There was, but he had never yet given us a straight answer to anything. He was another relative, an alcoholic. She said, "Ring him." I objected, but she insisted, "Ring him." So I did, not even expecting him to be there at that time.

To my great surprise, my cousin answered. He was indeed at home. I said to him, "Larry, not his real name, wants to come home."

My cousin immediately answered, "Bring him."

I said, "Lenny, you don't understand. He wants to come home and spend some time with us."

"What are you worried about? The room? I'll have it all made up by the time you get here."

I was struck with amazement. I couldn't believe that Lenny had answered me like that. So I thought, "Let me ask the Lord for a word."

My friend told me I was wasting time, "Just do it, that's what God wills." I couldn't believe it. I took up the Bible and asked the Lord to give me the word. I can't remember where it was in the Bible, but what I read was in essence this: "The Lord said to Moses, 'That which you are to do, go and do quickly for I am with you.'"

It was clear God was in this. I took the man home. My cousin, Lenny, had done exactly as he promised. He had the room prepared. Everything was ready. As the evening progressed, I realized that I had to help Larry to dress and to bathe. At times, during his stay, he wanted to go to the sea and I had to take him there and help him. I prayed continually, asking the Lord to help me to do this. I explained to Larry that I was no longer a wife to him. Our relationship had to be one of good friends, or like that of a brother and sister. He said he understood.

After I had him dressed for bed, he asked me to stay with him. I did and we talked into the hours of the night. We talked and we shared. He asked me to recount for him the things that had happened that had hurt me. He said he didn't understand how he could have done those things.

The next morning, there was a whole sense of peace and joy and fullness of love. I realized that the sharing and understanding we experienced was what I would have given my eye teeth for when we were married. It was a joy to fix his breakfast. As he ate, everything pleased him. It had not been like that when we were young! At that time there was nothing you could please him with. Everything was too sweet, too hot, too cold, not cooked enough or overcooked. I was continually under reproach. I could hardly believe how wonderful things now were.

I looked after him for four weeks. I took him to the sea and to the doctor, and we prayed together and read Scripture together. It was four weeks that looked like twenty years of companionship that I had always hoped we could have had.

One day a friend telephoned to say she had heard that I was seen with a man on a cane who looked like my husband. I told her it was and he was staying with me. She said, "In your house?" I said, "Yes," and she blurted out, "Babsie, are you crazy? How could you do a thing like that?" I told her this had been a gift from God to me. A tremendous grace had come to me and a healing had taken place.

One of my brothers came to the house, saw Larry, and left abruptly to complain to my sister that I had Larry in my home. My sister told him, "Just who said, 'I will,' Babsie or you?" My brother came right back to the house to see what he could do to help me care for Larry.

So, the whole family experienced a healing. The day before Larry left us, when I was getting things ready for him to leave, I had a sudden sense of panic. In those two weeks, I had continued with my routine of going where I had to go, but when I came home, he would be waiting for me and looking so happy when I came home. That was an experience I never had in the eight years we were married.

"Lord," I said, "my life has been interrupted. I wonder if I can go back to my old routine." I felt as though the Lord was present to me and I heard him speak in my heart, "Did you ever dream this could happen?" I told him no. "Don't you think I knew it all the time? Will you leave the rest to me?" Immediately, I experienced total peace.

Larry left. I put him on the plane and made sure he was comfortable and was cared for. When he left, my life just picked up again, like waters closing after the passing of a ship. It was as if I had dreamed all this. My life just flowed—except that I *had lost the burden of the grudge I had borne against that man and carried for twenty years. My gratitude to God knew no bounds. The healing was total.* The Lord had arranged it all himself. If you were to ask me now about the things that happened, I would have to tell you honestly, I have forgotten. I no longer remember. They are no more.

God really heals. He can help us learn to forgive and to forget. As Paul tells us, "Be transformed by the renewal of your mind, that you may discern what is the will of God, what is good and pleasing and perfect" (Rm 12:2). Part of this renewal of the mind is the power to forgive and forget for that is indeed "good and pleasing and perfect."

Questions for Reflection

1. Did anyone ever try to discourage you from forgiving another person? If so, how did you respond in that situation?
2. Did Auntie Babsie's honesty in this chapter cause you any uneasiness? Did it help you face a problem in your own life? If not too personal or painful, share with a friend.
3. If you still feel guilty over an already confessed and forgiven sin, ask the Holy Spirit to heal you of this problem. Such lingering guilt is not what God wants.

CHAPTER TEN

The Holy Spirit,
Author of Prayer

WHEN WE HAVE BEEN RENEWED AND REFRESHED by the Holy Spirit of God and when we have surrendered heart, mind and soul to God, our whole prayer lives change. The prayer of the heart replaces the prayer that flows merely from habit cultivated in early childhood or the mere need to pray because we have needs we want God to satisfy.

As we respond to the Spirit, we enter new realms of prayer. We come to realize that we pray from the heart and we pray with Jesus, in Jesus and through Jesus.

Our own prayers of petition give way to praise and to worship and adoration. As the Holy Spirit reveals Jesus to us, and we gaze in wonder and awe at his majesty, dignity and perfection, it is impossible not to exclaim, as did St. Thomas, "My Lord and my God!" From there we break forth into the prayer of praise. Praise is dependent on our knowledge of Jesus. As we know him more intimately, we spend more time declaring how wonderful he is. A litany of praise for his goodness flows spontaneously from our hearts.

By the power of the Holy Spirit, we come to know him as he is described by his various titles—Savior, Deliverer and Lord of our lives. As we gradually yield to Jesus through the invitation and action of the Holy Spirit, we come to call him Master, Mighty Healer, Faithful God, Lord of Life, Lord of the Universe, Creator King. The litany has no end.

Apart from those titles revealed in Scripture, when we come to know Jesus personally we give him our own titles, such as "Faithful Friend." We talk to him as we talk to a human companion with whom we feel a deep affinity. A love affair begins between us and Jesus. That deep love is akin to love of a husband and wife who have entered into a perfect unity of mind, soul, spirit and body and who have truly become one.

When the soul reaches this union with Christ, it is possible to respond to St. Paul's instruction to pray all the time, to make every moment of our lives a prayer. When we are at work with our minds and hands, our hearts can be filled with prayer and praise of God. In fact, when the Spirit unites us to Jesus in this way, we begin to see that all we do in the course of daily life, at work and at play, can become a prayer of praise to God.

When we work, as Pope John Paul II has said many times, we express the creativeness of God who has made us in his image. When we return kindness for insult, we express the saving love of Christ. When we console a sad person, we share the healing power of Jesus Christ. When we forgive, we invite people into the saving power of Christ. Even little things, like pulling weeds in a flower garden, as St. Theresa of the Child Jesus has shown us so well, can become powerful prayers of praise and thanksgiving: "We marvel at the wisdom of our God!"

When a person is so united to Jesus, it is not unusual that he wake up at night from a deep sleep with his heart praying the same prayer that he prayed all day. In that night-time awakening, the first word that comes to his lips is a word of prayer of wonder, of praise, of awe, of gratitude to the God who is so wonderful, beautiful, powerful, compassionate, forgiving and loving.

We recognize that this great God has kept his promise to be with us until the end of time. Our prayer is not perfected until, in a time of danger or serious difficulty, the first words of prayer that break forth from our lips are "Dear Jesus!" The first person we want to call is Jesus. Only then can we truly realize what the saints meant when they talked about living in Christ.

The Perfect Prayer

Prayer is indeed a gift from God to help us express our love and need for him. When we have truly received that gift, we realize that for years we may have merely mouthed the words of prayers. For example, we may have *said* the "Our Father" without recognizing, in that prayer, a complete and perfect formula for prayer.

In the Our Father, the perfect prayer that Jesus taught us to pray, we find several specific attitudes and a certain order that are essential to prayer.

"Our Father ..." From the first words of this prayer we come to recognize that God is indeed the Father of all of us, the Creator of all things. We are indeed creatures; but more than that—we are children of a concerned and loving Father. "Abba!" "Daddy!"

With St. Francis, we can look upon all creation as fellow creatures and upon other human beings as true brothers and sisters. We stand before this God, not merely as individuals, but each of us as members of a huge, huge family, the family of God. We stand in his presence with a host of witnesses. So, we pray *our* Father and not *my* Father.

The Holy Spirit frees us from ourselves to recognize that we are part of this huge family of man that is indeed from the Father and, through Jesus, called to return to him.

Hallowed be Thy name ... As we come to a deep, deep understanding of God as Father, we grasp with the whole intensity of our being that this Father is Lord of all. The second line of this prayer reminds us that his name is to be exalted, his honor guarded. Because he is so holy, he is to be glorified.

When Jesus asked us to pray, *"Hallowed be Thy name,"* he was asking us to become instruments through which the name of God can be proclaimed as holy and exalted continually.

This exaltation of the name of God is a powerful sword to defeat the devil, who seeks to blaspheme and to destroy the honor of our God who is forever faithful. Thanksgiving and praise are the way to enter into the presence of God. As the psalmist tells us, "Enter his gates with thanksgiving" and "his courts with praise" (Ps 100:4).

Many Christians have always given thanks to God for what he has done, for answering this or that prayer. But we must give thanks not for what God *has done* but for *who he is!* We praise him for simply being God. His majesty and his divine nature are reason enough to praise him and to thank him for letting us know him. Imagine! Mere creatures able to know their Creator, the Father of all life!

Praise is a higher form of prayer than thanksgiving. Because we praise him even before he has done anything, even when we feel, in those weak moments, that he has not answered our prayers!

When we come to know God this intimately, we recognize how puny we are compared with him. We recognize our tainted nature and our weaknesses. But at the same time, we realize how blessed we are that this magnificent God knows and loves each one of us personally. Our hearts overflow with appreciation for that great goodness and that awesome divinity, that God who has no beginning and no end. That is awesome!

Appreciation escalates into praise. Is it not true that when someone is good to us we appreciate it? And, in appreciation, we often tell that person, "How good you are!" Is that not praise? How much more does the Spirit-filled heart look upon God and tell him, "How good you are! How great you are! How beautiful you are! Oh, God, how mighty you are! How compassionate and loving! How marvelous! How divine! How gracious and patient! Oh, God! Oh, God! Oh, God!" Sometimes, our praise can only be expressed in those two words, "Oh, God!" We praise him for who he is! Praise is an exalted form of prayer; as the Scriptures tell us, "Thou art holy, enthroned on the praises of Israel" (Ps 22:3, RSV).

"Thy kingdom come ..." God's kingdom includes all of creation. Everything belongs to God. Sin has disrupted the kingdom. We were separated from God by sin. Jesus reunites us to the Father through his passion, death and resurrection. Jesus makes it possible for us to be reunited with the Father, to intercede and look forward to the fulfillment of the kingdom of God on earth. In Jesus and through his Church, the kingdom is already here but not yet completely visible.

In his encyclical, *Redemptoris Missio,* Pope John Paul II writes, "The Kingdom of God cannot be detached either from Christ of from the Church ... the Church is ordered toward the kingdom, of which she is the seed, sign, and instrument. (chapter 2, The Kingdom of God, #18). The kingdom will become expressly visible when the King, Jesus Christ, is established in the hearts of all men by conversion and repentance. His

Holiness continues, "In a word, the kingdom of God is the manifestation and the realization of God's plan of salvation in all its fulness" (#15).

The prophet Isaiah gives a wonderful and exciting picture of the kingdom of God: "Then the wolf will be a guest of the lamb, and the leopard shall lie down with the kid; The calf and the young lion shall browse together, with a little child to guide them. The cow and the bear shall be neighbors, together their young shall rest; the lion shall eat hay like the ox. The baby shall play by the cobra's den, and the child lay his hand on the adder's lair. There shall be no harm or ruin on all my holy mountain; for the earth shall be filled with knowledge of the Lord, as water covers the seas" (Is 11:6-9).

I never fail to chuckle as I conceive the wolf being a guest of the lamb and not praying in his heart the grace before meals. Truly that will be a wonderful era when all men live in unity, filled with the love of God in their hearts, protected by kingdom laws and enjoying together all the kingdom provisions that have been established by the Father through Jesus Christ the Son.

"Thy will be done ..." When we pray, motivated and fueled by the Holy Spirit for *God's will to be done*, our one and only goal is just that—*God's will*. Nothing less than God's will is acceptable to the prayerful heart.

God's will was all that our Lord Jesus pursued, even in Gethsemane, as he faced a terrible, torturous death. Someone once said, "God writes straight on crooked lines." Another way of putting it is, "Only God can bring good from evil." The crucifixion of Jesus was the most evil deed ever born in the human heart. Yet, because of the obedience of Jesus, the new Adam,

God offers salvation to the world through this most horrible evil.

Our loving Father, our all-loving and mighty God, would never do anything that was not for our perfect good. He sees all that has happened and will happen to us, and all that we did and will do. He sees us on our deathbed, and will do nothing to us that will turn us from him in that final hour. His will for us is perfect. He wills us to pass from this life to the next in his loving arms. Our Father would never give us a stone when we ask for bread. Nor would he give us a scorpion when we ask for an egg! We join our wills with his, then, and pray that his will be done.

"Give us this day ..." Dependence on God for life itself and the food we need, both for our bodies and our souls, is expressed by Jesus when he tells us to pray, "Give us this day *our daily bread.*" As we advance in prayer, we become deeply conscious of the fact that God has provided for us all the food we need to live in the bread of his holy Word. Most importantly, he has provided us the Bread of Life in Holy Communion. We receive the Eucharist, the Body and Blood of Jesus Christ, which heals and consoles us and prepares us to be strong. Holy Communion sanctifies us. The Eucharist, as our spiritual nourishment, gives us the grace to develop a wholesome attitude toward God, others and ourselves.

"And forgive us our trespasses ..." Contrition is another inherent part of prayer. Jesus shows us we must be contrite, we must ask for forgiveness. He says, "*Forgive us our trespasses as we forgive those who trespass against us.*" We ask to be forgiven for our pettiness, weaknesses and inadequacies, whatever they may be. We

ask to be forgiven for those sins we commit out of selfishness and pride. We have the confidence that we are forgiven when we seek God's mercy.

The Holy Spirit helps us understand what the saints meant when they cried out, "Of all sinners, I am the worst!" As they grew in their knowledge and love of God, they began to see more clearly how their sins were an affront to God, an insult to whom they were called to be. They saw the gravity of their sins in the light of the goodness of God. They were led not only to repent and make amends for their own sins, but many of them led lives of prayer and sacrifice in reparation for the sins of the world. Their voluntary sacrifices were a way to tell God, "Oh, God! You do not deserve to be treated this way. You are so good and so holy! Forgive us all, Lord, for our sins!" Such a life of repentance for the sins of the world reflects, like a mirror, what happened on the cross: Jesus took on all the sins of the world and died so we might all be saved.

"Deliver us from evil ..." Temptation is a constant companion of the faith-filled heart. Jesus, in his prayer, teaches us to ask for deliverance in temptation. This does not mean that temptation will cease. No, it means that we depend on God to give us the strength to turn our backs on temptation and flee to the protective embrace of Jesus.

A Christian must never attempt to fight Satan and thus deal with temptation on his own. Why fight a battle that has already been won? No, do not fight a needless battle. Fly to the Victor. Fly to Christ. Praise him in the face of temptation. *God inhabits the praise of his people.* If someone offends you and you are tempted to get angry and retaliate in kind, rather just praise

Jesus: "Jesus! You are so good, so compassionate, understanding, kind and forgiving! Praise you, Jesus, for your goodness and for your victory!"

If you begin immediately to praise, even while you feel anger and resentment in your heart, God will inhabit your praise and the devil will have to flee and take his temptation with him. He cannot stand to be in God's presence!

The Perfect Prayer of the Mass

We have already said that the Our Father is a perfect model for prayer. The Church tells us that the Mass is also a perfect prayer. All those elements we find in the Our Father are present in Holy Mass.

We begin the Mass with the sign of the cross. This acknowledges we are children of the Father, disciples and brothers and sisters of the Son, and sanctuaries of the Holy Spirit. Our whole lives are entwined in the life of the Trinity as we reflectively make the sign of the cross.

We profess that God is Three Persons, but one and only one God. This is the primal doctrine of our faith. God is one. There are Three Persons who are each individually fully God, but God is one. There is only one divine nature which is fully possessed by each of the Three Persons of the Blessed Trinity, Father, Son and Holy Spirit. We bless ourselves with the sign of our redemption. We bless ourselves with the sign of our baptism and we remember the awful price paid by God to make us his children again.

The very next thing in the Mass is admission and confession of sin. We ask God's pardon. We are in need of his saving grace. We then feast on the Word of God. The Word is our daily bread as is the Eucharist. The Word of God becomes bread of life for us. As the precious Word of God is broken—or preached—we embrace his revelation and ask that his kingdom come and his gracious will be done on earth as it is in heaven. And this desire is voiced later in the Mass as we pray together the Our Father.

Then we have the transformation of the bread and wine into the Body and Blood of Jesus. This happens only through the power of the Holy Spirit. The priest prays, asking God to let his Spirit come upon the gifts so they can be made holy and become the Body and Blood of Jesus Christ. This bread and wine come to us from God's providence in nature and through the work of human hands. Then, by the power of the Spirit, these gifts are transformed into the real presence of Jesus. We receive our daily bread, the Bread of Life. We become one with Christ in receiving communion and we can pray with Jesus in the will of God. We ask God to protect us and deliver us from temptation and from all evil.

And finally, we thank God and go on our way to bring the fruit of the Mass into our daily lives, our relationships, work and play. So, the Holy Mass is indeed a perfect prayer which the Spirit calls us to pray even daily in union with the Church throughout the world.

The Spirit Comes to Our Aid

When we try to pray privately, it is at times difficult to know how to pray, or for what to pray. The Spirit comes to our aid. Our faith grows by hearing the Word of God and by praying in the Spirit. "But you, beloved, build yourselves up in your most holy faith; pray in the Holy Spirit" (Jude 1:20a).

To hear the word of God, in this biblical sense, is to listen with an open and faithful heart and to obey God's word. For us Catholics, it means embracing the Church's interpretations of Scripture and its doctrine and moral teachings. To pray in the Spirit is to be open to the Spirit's promptings, to let the Spirit of God pray in us, with us and for us. We surely pray ourselves, but we pray in obedience to God's will, with Jesus and in his submission to the Father's will, and under the guidance and inspiration of the Holy Spirit.

Prayer, then, becomes a way of life. It flows from the heart, from the very "guts" of our baptized souls where the Holy Spirit dwells. And so we come to realize that true prayer is initiated by the Holy Spirit and we are instruments of prayer. *Our prayer rises to God like a fragrant offering when it is uttered from and in his Spirit,* and this can happen twenty-four hours a day if we are sensitive to the Holy Spirit within us. Anyone who aspires to true prayer will invoke the Holy Spirit's help to walk constantly in the anointing of God.

Walking in the Spirit's Anointing

What does it mean, to walk in God's anointing? It means to be filled with the Holy Spirit, to surrender oneself to the will of God, to experience the presence, power and love of God, to be filled with joy as a child of God.

In and under this anointing, we become channels of anointing for others. Wherever we are, whatever is lacking in the body of Christ, we can be used by God as an avenue of his grace. We can pray with St. Francis from the depths of our hearts: "Where there is hatred, let me bring your love. Where there is injury, pardon. Where there is despair, hope. Where there is darkness, light." The prayer becomes more than words, when we are walking in the light and power of the Holy Spirit. It becomes a reality. We become instruments of God's love, of his forgiveness and of the hope which rests in our faith in Christ.

We live this beautiful life. We have been transformed, renewed and refreshed by the Spirit and we are used by the Spirit, even when we are not aware of being a good witness for Christ. We seek not *to be loved*. Rather we seek *to love!* We don't seek *to be consoled* and *to be understood*, but *to be a source* of consolation and understanding. Suddenly our hearts see the needs of others and are prompted to respond.

Special Ways and Times to Pray

For many generations, the Church has called us to special ways in which to pray and to special times for prayer.

The Angelus. When people worked in the fields, the church bells would ring at six A.M., twelve noon, and six P.M. People stopped immediately, regardless of their condition and frame of mind, to reflect on the mystery of the Incarnation. In this time of recollection, they realized they were more than beasts of burden. They were children of God. They made the sign of the cross at the ringing of the bell, realized they were mysteriously and wondrously united to God, to the Blessed Trinity. And they prayed:

> *The angel of the Lord declared unto Mary and she conceived of the Holy Spirit.... Hail Mary, full of grace, the Lord is with thee. Blessed art thou among women and blessed is the fruit of thy womb, Jesus. Holy Mary, mother of God, pray for us sinners, now and at the hour of our death. Amen.*

Behold the handmaid of the Lord; be it done unto me according to thy word. (Hail Mary, etc.)

And the word became flesh and dwelt among us. (Hail Mary, etc.)

Pray for us, O Holy Mother of God, that we may be made worthy of the promises of Christ.

Let us pray: Pour forth, we beseech thee, O Lord, thy grace into our hearts that we to whom the incarnation of Christ thy Son was made known by the message of an angel, may by his passion and cross be brought to the glory of his resurrection through the same Christ, our Lord. Amen.

If we stop to repeat this prayer three times a day, reflectively, we will better understand who we are and what was done for us in Christ by the power of the Holy Spirit. The Church wants us to realize, through this prayer, that the call he made to Mary is our call as well. The Word became flesh in Mary's womb. It must become flesh in our hearts. We remember our mighty God *asks* us. Our gracious God patiently awaits our reply. "Be it done unto me, Lord, according to your will!"

Like Mary, we become the instruments to bring Jesus into the world in our own time and place. We become tabernacles of his holy presence. We should be so full of Jesus, so full of grace that people will know we love God and say to us, as we say to Mary, "Please pray for us." The closer we come to Christ, the more we are transformed into his image, the more we become intercessors for others.

The Rosary. Another popular prayer that has touched millions over many generations is the Rosary. Through this ancient prayer, we move with Mary through the life of Christ. This beautiful meditation on the life of Jesus is divided into fifteen reflections, fifteen decades (or groups of beads) that prompt us to pray the Our Father, ten Hail Marys and the Glory Be. At the end of each decade a brief prayer is said asking for God's mercy.

As we pray each decade, we contemplate one of the fifteen "mysteries" in the life of Christ which he shared so intimately with his Blessed Mother. Those mysteries are divided into three groups—the joyful, sorrowful and glorious mysteries.

Each set of five mysteries begins with the Creed, an Our Father, three Hail Marys and the doxology, "Glory be to the Father and to the Son and to the Holy Spirit, as it was in the beginning, is now and will be forever."

THE JOYFUL MYSTERIES

(See Lk 1:1-2:52)

These mysteries call us to reflect on how Archangel Gabriel announced the coming of the Lord to Mary, the birth of Jesus and his early years.

First Joyful Mystery: The Annunciation. Here we contemplate the coming of the angel to the Virgin Mary. "Hail, full of grace, the Lord is with you!" proclaims the angel. He tells Mary she is to have a Son who will be conceived by the Holy Spirit. He will be the Son of God. She responds in faith with her now famous words, "Behold, I am the handmaid of the Lord. May it be done to me according to your word" (Lk 1:38). We may ask God as we pray this mystery for that kind of faith and willingness to do God's will.

Second Joyful Mystery: The Visitation. Mary, now carrying the Christ Child in her womb, visits her elderly cousin, Elizabeth, who herself is pregnant with her own first child, later to be known as John the Baptist. When Mary calls, the infant in Elizabeth's womb leaps for joy.

Elizabeth proclaims: "Blessed are you among women and blessed is the fruit of your womb!" As we pray, we might ask God for Mary's charity toward others and for Elizabeth's ready willingness to see God's hand in mystery. The gift the Holy Spirit has placed in our hearts is not one to be kept in isolation, but one to be shared. As the fruit of the Spirit grow in us, we give them away.

Third Joyful Mystery: The Birth of our Lord, Jesus Christ. We enter with Mary into the stable in Bethlehem. We become conscious that our hearts could be like a stable, but when Jesus enters, the stable is transformed into a tabernacle. We all know the beautiful Christmas story from Luke. He is among the poor. Shepherds come. We are grateful for his presence in our lives, for his coming as one of us, like us in all things but sin. We pray that God give us the grace to be humble and simple and to embrace the poor.

Fourth Joyful Mystery: The Presentation. Joseph and Mary, according to their Jewish religious tradition, take the small child to the temple where he is to be dedicated to God. It is a moment of joy, but one of stark reality. Among all the children in the temple that day, Mary's child is singled out. The prophet Simeon declares that the babe is the Messiah. He prophesies that Jesus will cause many to rise and fall and that a sword will pierce Mary's own heart.

We, who are renewed in the Spirit, bear the mark of this sword through our own hearts. We mourn with Jesus the sufferings and the sins of the world. We must each give life, hope and joy to the world through our own prophetic word, as we live the life of the Spirit and share our faith in Jesus. Here we pray for that grace. We also might pray for the grace to present ourselves, our families, all our work and all we hold dear to God for his blessing and dedicate all to his use.

Fifth Joyful Mystery: The Finding of Jesus in the Temple. On their journey from Jerusalem, the twelve-year-old Jesus was discovered to be missing from the group traveling with his parents. Joseph and Mary return to Jerusalem. They search for him high and low. For three days they search among family and friends. Finally they search in the temple. It is there that they find him.

In this mystery we learn from Mary to seek Jesus with all our hearts, in the high and low places of our lives, in the good news and the bad. It is impossible for us to live without him. As we continue to seek Jesus, we discover more and more of him— friend, philosopher, the source of all knowledge and wisdom. In the long run, he is always to be found in the assembly of the faithful.

When his parents asked Jesus why he caused them so much fear and pain, his response puzzled them: "Did you not know I had to be about my Father's business?" As we meditate on this mystery, we might ask God to make us a temple of his presence, to keep us faithfully united to his Church and to help us always seek the wisdom of truly holy people—and to be about our Father's business.

THE SORROWFUL MYSTERIES

(See Lk 22:39-24:56)

It doesn't take long for us to realize that to live in the Spirit often means alienation from certain people, even from some family members. There is joy in living the life of the Spirit, but there are also sorrows. An example of this happened years ago in Trinidad when a young seminarian was leading us in Scripture study and prayer.

Some of us were baptized in the Spirit. At the time the seminarian had been on leave, and so did not have this same experience. It was not long before we began to drift apart. Somehow the friendship became strained. We were no longer on the same wavelength. We were at loggerheads when we tried to plan, pray or teach together. We couldn't understand it. Although we shared faith in Jesus Christ, something was now different. As he said years later, before he experienced the baptism of the Holy Spirit and began to live the life in the Spirit, we were thinking on two different levels. So, even within the joy of a faith community, pain and sorrow can result.

There is a funny story about a young man who wanted to be a priest. His father objected: "Why can't you be like your brothers and everybody else and get married and have children?"

The boy shot back, "If I have decided to walk with Jesus, why do you object?" A little while later, the son went to the father and said, "I need to go to a meeting. May I borrow the car?"

The father shot back, "You have decided to walk with Jesus, so you can walk to your meeting." And so he did.

To follow Christ means self-denial. It means the cross. So, the sorrowful mysteries.

First Sorrowful Mystery: The Agony in the Garden. Jesus had come to the end of his public demonstration of power, his preaching about love and his healing ministry. He knew what remained was the cross. His very life would have to be given if the world would be redeemed. He had celebrated the Last Supper and instituted the Eucharist. Now, we see Jesus in Gethsemane. He foresees the price he must pay for the salvation of souls. He cringes from it. He cries out, "Father, Father, if it is possible let this cup pass from me!" But he perseveres: "Thy will, not mine, be done." He repeated his plea to the Father several times.

From this mystery we learn that we should persevere in prayer. Like Jesus, when the anointing of the Spirit comes, we will have the strength to accept God's will no matter what it is. Mary herself had to yield again to the Father and again state her "fiat." She had to yield her Son to the cross for the sake of the world. We learn to yield with Mary as we pray this mystery of the Rosary. We ask the Lord to give us the deepest possible desire to embrace God's will regardless of the cost. We pray for obedience.

Second Sorrowful Mystery: The Scourging at the Pillar. Jesus was wounded for our transgressions, and by his stripes we are healed. Jesus asked for no quarter. He received all forty stripes. He received both the scourging and death on the cross for our sins. Jesus was brutally beaten with whips. The scourging stopped when a person was barely left alive. His innocent flesh was torn by the whipping and he bled and suffered for us.

Mary was helpless in the face of her Son's suffering.

Sometimes we find ourselves helpless, too, and we, as did Mary, accept suffering because of the anointing of the Spirit. We pray for purity of mind, heart and body. We pray for those who suffer for the sake of truth. We pray for healing of body and soul.

Third Sorrowful Mystery: The Crowning with Thorns. It was not enough to beat this innocent man almost to death. Not enough to so torture the man who is also God. Now they mock him, cruelly shoving a crown of sharp thorns on his head and bowing before him saying derisively, "Hail, King of the Jews." Although done in jest and cruel mockery, it was these pagan soldiers who first said aloud that Jesus was a king. Jesus is indeed King of Kings and Lord of Lords, yet he endured this mockery for our sake.

We share in the royalty of Jesus; like Jesus we also sometimes suffer abuse and mockery for our faith, or just for being different from others in status, race and culture. We accept this as Jesus did, for the sake of those who hurt us. We offer our pain for their salvation. We pray for humility and for the gifts of long-suffering and unconditional love when we are abused by others.

Fourth Sorrowful Mystery: Jesus Carries the Cross. We cannot escape the cross. The Christian comes to realize that the cross must be embraced. The Lord Jesus is burdened by the heavy cross. In his weakened state, he is near death. A stranger is forced to help him carry his cross. Simon of Cyrene grudgingly helps Jesus with the cross.

Sometimes we resent people, because of our pride, who help us grudgingly. But Jesus looked at Simon with gratitude because, however unwilling, Simon's help enabled Jesus to reach Calvary, where the work of redemption would be finished. Jesus walks to his death, a public death, the death of a criminal. The streets are filled with jeering crowds, taunting him. His disciples have left him, except for his Mother, two other women and young John.

We pray for perseverance as we endure our own crosses in life. We pray for the grace to help others in their times of difficulty. We pray for those who help us either joyfully or grudgingly. We could never be where we are today without the many Simons that Jesus has provided for us.

Fifth Sorrowful Mystery: The Crucifixion. Jesus totally abandons himself to the will of the Father. This death was his confrontation with the hideousness of sin. He who had never sinned was swallowed up by the sin of the world. He was so swallowed up by the evil of sin that in the darkness of his soul he cried out, "Father! Why have you abandoned me?" However, by the power of the Spirit, Jesus, who was truly a man nailed naked to that cross, was able to say, "Father, into your hands I commend my spirit."

This final act of obedience and worship, this saving act of Jesus, was done at a crossroads where the world passed by— and it was written up in every language for all to see, "Jesus of Nazareth, King of the Jews." Again, it was in jest, but it was a proclamation of truth.

In the midst of his suffering, Jesus utters an almost unbelievable prayer for someone so victimized by evil: "Father, forgive them, for they know not what they do." And he gives an unbelievable gift to us. He tells John: "This is your Mother." And he tells Mary, his Mother, "This is your son." The Church has held from the beginning that Mary is our Mother because Jesus gave her to us through "the beloved disciple." Also, since we are brothers and sisters of Christ, then we are sons and daughters not only of his Father but of his Mother as well. We pray for total consecration to Jesus. We pray for the grace to die to self for the love of Christ. We pray for the willingness to expand our hearts, as Mary did, to include all who are given to us by God.

THE GLORIOUS MYSTERIES

(See Luke 24:1-50; Acts 1:1-14, 2:1-41)

St. Thérèse of the Child Jesus had a great gift of understanding. She was never moved by the praises of men or the glory anyone wanted to heap upon her. She was never threatened by the criticisms or barbs thrown her way.

Sometimes, very humble people who are lifted up in honor in public cringe from the attention, but in humility bear it without pride or presumption. We should become ever more humble when we receive gifts from God because we can truthfully say it is not *we who are gifted* but *God is the gift* and *he gives us a share of himself* for his own good purposes. The real glory comes when we rejoice in the glory of the Lord.

First Glorious Mystery: The Resurrection. Alleluia! Jesus is risen from the dead! He comes out of the tomb and says "BOOOO!" and Satan runs away in terror. Satan thought it was over, that he had won. He forgot that it was Jesus who said, as he died on the cross, "It is finished!" Jesus finished his work. Not Satan. Jesus is victor, not Satan. Satan is defeated, not Jesus.

Jesus is risen! Not *has* risen. He *is* risen! He is alive and well.

His resurrection is as real for us today as it was for those stunned disciples on that first Easter Sunday. In fact, the apostles couldn't rejoice in the Resurrection. They were so frightened they ran and hid. They had abandoned Jesus and now they were afraid he had come to pay them back. They only needed the gift of repentance rather than make excuses for themselves. And apparently they had that gift because when Jesus appeared to them, he gave them peace instead of pain. With them, we repent and then rejoice in the Resurrection.

Whenever we meet Christ with repentance, we experience deep joy and freedom from guilt. It is a resurrection experience. We come to realize that all life is death and resurrection. *Out of every experience of crucifixion comes the glory of resurrection.* As we come out of sorrow, we enter into exultant joy. God has been faithful. He has done for us what he has done for Jesus.

The same Spirit who raised Christ from the dead lives in us, and he will raise us up every time we are down. The resurrection of Jesus seals the Paschal Mystery, the mystery of our redemption by the only Son of God. It is the resurrection of Jesus as well as his passion and death that redeem us. In baptism, we die with Christ and also rise with him. On Easter Sunday, and in every Mass throughout the year, we celebrate this wonderful mystery in great joy.

We, too, recognize him in the breaking of the bread. We speak of new life, of everlasting life. We dance for joy because Jesus has overcome both sin and death. His resurrection is a seal to our faith in him as Son of God, as Messiah, Savior, Redeemer. As we say the Our Father and the Hail Marys, as we move our fingers over the beads, we pray for the gift of faith, the kind of faith that leads us to live and die and rise for Jesus.

Second Glorious Mystery: The Ascension. Jesus, after some time with his apostles and disciples after he rose from the dead, ascends into heaven. We read in the Gospel of Matthew his final words to the disciples:

> "Go, therefore, and make disciples of all nations, baptizing them in the name of the Father, and of the Son, and of the holy Spirit, teaching them to observe all that I have commanded you. And behold, I am with you always, until the end of the age." MATTHEW 28:19-20

The apostles stood in rapture, gazing at Jesus ascending into heaven. Maybe they felt abandoned and afraid, because Jesus sent them an angel who asked them why they were standing around gazing into the heavens. He said that Jesus would come again from heaven in glory. "While he is gone," he said to them, "you have a job to do." Jesus had given them a clear command: Go and teach, baptize. We realize we have the commission to pass on the faith. That's our commission from baptism.

While on earth, before and after his death and ascension, Jesus told us many things—he was going away to prepare a place for us, he would send us the Holy Spirit to comfort us, we would do all he did and even more for the sake of souls. As we contemplate Jesus' ascension to his Father, we may pray for the gift of hope, hope in the promises of Jesus who stays with us even while he is at the Father's right hand. We pray for grace to evangelize.

Third Glorious Mystery: The Coming of the Holy Spirit. What glory! The Spirit comes! The Church is born! Suddenly, the disciples were no longer hiding and silenced in fear. They now had the boldness of faith. They were transformed, as Jesus promised, by the power of the Spirit.

Mary stayed with the apostles, in the Upper Room and at Pentecost. She had known the fullness of the power of the Spirit. She knew Jesus and knew he would indeed do what he said he would do, namely, to send the Holy Spirit. She had total and absolute confidence in her Son's promise.

The Spirit came to them as tongues of fire and a strong rushing wind. Peter was so eloquent that three thousand people were converted to Christ that first Pentecost. The Spirit was so eloquent that people of many nations heard the message in their own tongues!

As we reflect on the coming of the Holy Spirit, we recommit ourselves to carry out the mission of Jesus. We ask for the grace to be faithful as Mary was faithful. This is the last we hear of Mary. She is not even mentioned in the Acts of the Apostles. In fact, the last words we hear from her lips were uttered long before, at Cana, when she told servants at a wedding to listen to Jesus. Her exact words were, "Do whatever he tells you." And that is good advice for all of us. We must do whatever Jesus tells us.

We pray, during this mystery, for full surrender to the power and love of the Holy Spirit, to be at last fully transformed, ourselves and all Christians, into the perfect image of Christ.

Fourth Glorious Mystery: The Assumption. The Church has held from its earliest days that Mary, conceived without original sin and preserved from sin all her life, was taken body and soul into heaven to be with her beloved Son. Her body never saw corruption.

Many people seem to have difficulty accepting this teaching of the Church. But we know that nothing is impossible with God. We do have the scriptural precedent of Elijah being taken up into heaven. Enoch was taken up. Why should we doubt that the person who had been most instrumental in bringing our Savior into the world could be given such a gift by God?

This doctrine is not in Scripture, but the Church teaches this doctrine with the same authority, she teaches what is and what is not the inspired Word of God. Mary goes before us, following Jesus. Jesus is her Son and her Lord, just as he is our brother and our Lord. Mary needed Jesus for her own salvation. She was conceived sinless due to the merits Jesus would win for us all. If God had not made this provision for Mary, then Jesus would have been brought up in the shadow of sin.

God is not limited by time and space. He knew what merits Jesus would win for us and he applied them to Mary as she was conceived in her mother's womb. That's what we mean by the Immaculate Conception. During this mystery, we pray for our own arrival in heaven. We desire eternal life with God. We contemplate the joy of our Triune God as Mary, the new Eve, follows Jesus, the new Adam, into the eternal kingdom. We thank God for Mary's faith and holiness. We ask her to pray with us and for us, that we may also be holy and faithful and without sin when Jesus returns.

Fifth Glorious Mystery: The Crowning of Mary as Queen of Heaven. Finally, we celebrate with the whole family of God, the crowning of our Lady as Queen of Heaven. She is also known as Queen of Angels, of Apostles, of Martyrs, of Peace, of the whole universe. Again, this is not recorded in Scripture. It is the Church's teaching; it is devotional.

If Jesus is King, then Mary must be Queen and as Queen, she has a crown. Scripture promises us all a crown, "the crown of righteousness;" awaits us and "an unfading crown of glory" (see 2 Tm 4:8; 1 Pt 5:4; Rev 3:11). If we have a crown, most surely Mary, the Mother of Jesus, has the most beautiful crown of all.

We give Mary the title of Queen to honor both her and her Son. How it must please Jesus to see us love and honor the Mother he so loves, the Mother he gave to us as our own as he hung in agony on that terrible cross!

As we pray this mystery, we celebrate our own royalty. We are, after all, a royal priesthood and a holy nation. We pray for the dignity that should be ours as, resisting temptation, we shine forth as faithful, loyal princesses and princes in the kingdom of the Father. As coheirs of Christ, we inherit that eternal kingdom. We pray in thanksgiving for such generosity on the part of God to so sinful and ungrateful a people as we too often are.

So, there. The Rosary is a reflection of the life of Christ in a nutshell. It is a contemplative prayer, a prayer encouraged by the Church to draw us into the mystery of Mary and to help us desire the transformation, renewal and refreshment of the Holy Spirit as she so desired and received it for the sake of Christ. As we pray the Rosary contemplatively, we grasp that the life of Jesus is, in fact, also our life. Just as our lives have highlights of joy, depths of sorrow and flashes of glory, so Jesus' life had all these elements.

Jesus said that anyone who hears the word of God and keeps it is his mother, his brother and his sister (Mk 3:33). It is not presumptuous of us to say that God hopes each one of us will give birth to Christ and give him away to the world. At our baptisms, with the reception of the Holy Spirit, we have been commissioned to make Christ visible and to give him away to the rest of the world as Mary did. Mary was only able to do this through the power of the Holy Spirit. Jesus invites us also to accept the power of the Holy Spirit.

Questions for Reflection

1. The next time you go to church, spend some time before Mass thinking on the meaning of the Our Father. Reflect on how its attitudes are also contained in the Mass.
2. For one week only, make an effort to recite the Angelus with a friend at six A.M., twelve noon, and six P.M. After a week, share with one another what this has meant to you.
3. In what ways can you begin to make your prayer life one more of praise than petition? Discuss this with a friend or spiritual director.

CHAPTER ELEVEN

Getting to Know
and Love Mary

Who is this that comes forth like the dawn,
as beautiful as the moon, as resplendent as the sun,
as awe-inspiring as bannered troops?

SONG OF SONGS 6:10

TO LIVE AND REFRESH OUR LIVES IN THE SPIRIT, we must become like Mary, so open to God that Jesus can find a home in our hearts. When we have that kind of relationship with God, many problems and difficulties either disappear or we see them from an entirely different perspective.

Before I received the baptism of the Holy Spirit, I was suffering depression. I had to take lithium, one pill a day, to be able to function. But after the Spirit, I was filled with this buoyancy, a real joy. Depression was gone. I forgot all about lithium. In the twenty-five years since, I have never had to touch a tranquilizer or sleeping pill. The Lord be praised.

God had acted in my life and when I began to feel depressed, I remembered the admonition, "When God has acted, don't let the symptoms confuse you."

In this new-found life in the Spirit, I began to wonder about all the years before that I had spent praying all the popular devotions, especially all those Rosaries. Through it all, I had never felt that close to God, but now in an instant, the Spirit changed all that. I wondered about the Church's teachings on Mary and I began to question them. But one thing kept me going. I really believed what Jesus said, "I am with you always, even until the end of the world."

I realized how traditional was our devotion to Mary. I kept saying, "If God is with us, surely he could not have allowed us to carry on in error over all these years. So I decided to search the Church's traditions to see if I could find something that would question this Marian devotion.

I began to read all about the saints. I found that all of them had a devotion to Mary; on and on, generation after generation of the saints of the Church. The saints praised God for Mary and for the gifts of their devotion to her. Her faithful response to God sustained them all through their lives. This was very difficult for me since I had begun to be swayed by the Protestant sentiment that praying the Rosary was babbling nonsense and vain, repetitious prayers.

Yet, I could not abandon this habit of praying to Mary. To question in those days was to put yourself in a precarious position. I was being accused of rejecting Mary, when actually I was on an intense search for truth. People challenged me because I was speaking only about Jesus. I told them that Mary was taught every day in the Catholic Church. I felt that my ministry was to the lost sheep of the Catholic Church. I wanted to help them rediscover Jesus and the power of the Spirit. In a sense, this setting aside of Mary was a very common condition in the charismatic renewal and in other parts of the Church following Vatican Council II.

Since I was ministering to Catholics, I often found myself

leading in the Rosary since it is very dear to Catholics. But I just could not pray the Rosary as I had before entering into this new life. So, as I prayed the Rosary, I began to read the relevant Scriptures for each mystery. I invited them to meditate on the mysteries and to pray aloud their desires and intentions, and then we would pray the decade of prayers. We prayed slowly so each word could be heard and understood in our hearts. Actually, to the best of my knowledge, I was doing the scriptural Rosary before it had been printed! But it was the only way I could find solace in leading people in the Rosary.

One day, it struck me that I had known about Jesus all of my life, but the revelation of him to me personally came only with the release of the Spirit in my life. I never had a personal relationship with him until the Spirit filled me with new life. I began to think that perhaps Mary, too, had to be revealed to the faithful heart before one could understand her and the devotion the Church paid her. If Jesus was mystery, Mary, too, could be mystery.

"Lord, Show Me Mary"

I began to pray, "Lord, reveal to me the mystery of Mary." I would pray from the depth of my heart, because this problem with Mary challenged my relationship with the Church and my wholehearted response to Jesus and the Church.

One night, I was seated before the Blessed Sacrament. I found myself in conversation with Jesus. I was really pouring out my heart, so close did I feel to him. In the middle of this conversation, it suddenly struck me: I was talking to Jesus as though he were real, and he is real. But, how could I be so familiar? Maybe this was disrespectful and presumptuous. So, I apologized to Jesus and decided to take up my Bible to read something worthwhile. I asked Jesus to lead me to something in the Bible that he wanted me to read.

I took up my Bible, opened it. And it was opened at the first chapter of the Song of Songs. I had never read the entire book, so I decided to do so. As I read it, I came to chapter six, verse ten: *"Who is this who comes like the dawn...?"*

It was as though my eyes were glued to that passage. My spirit was lifted up. I felt exultation, and heard in my spirit the question, "Who is she?"

I said, "That's Mary."

Again, a nudge: "And who else?"

I said, "Well, Protestants say it is the Church."

Again the nudge: "And who else?"

I said, "I don't know."

And the answer came, "It is you, too."

I did not understand how I could be the beautiful one, but then I recalled that God said he had reserved for himself from age to age a people who blessed him. And I was part of that people. Wherever God's name is exalted and blessed, we are exalted and blessed because we are part of his body.

It was as if the Lord said to me, "My body was in Mary's womb, wasn't it? You are a member of my body. You were in Mary's womb."

So I said, "Yes!"

He said, "Are you sure?"

I said, "Yes!"

He said, "On the day of Pentecost when the Church was born, Mary was in the Church. You are in the Church. The Church is my body. Mary is in my body. You are in my body." He asked me, "Am I in your heart?"

I said, "Yes, Lord."

He said, "Well, if Mary is in my Body and I am in your heart, then Mary is in your heart."

Then I said, "Oh, my God!"

He said, "It's simple, Babsie, so very simple. It is all one—Mary in me, I in you, you in me, Mary in you and you in Mary. It is all one."

It was as though my whole consciousness expanded in an instant so I could take all this in. We are all one! All one! And we cannot deny any part of the body!

I continued to reflect on Mary. Some time later I went to Barbados for a conference. It was an ecumenical conference. All our bishops were there and many priests. I was supposed to give a talk on the Church. I spent two days preparing, but I just couldn't make any headway. My talk was at nine A.M. on a given morning. The night before, I went to bed very discouraged. I said to the Lord, "Look, I have to give this talk in the morning. You see how hard I've tried and I've come up with nothing. Unless you help me, Lord, it's a lost cause. I want to remind you, Lord, that I have nothing to lose. My reputation was shot twenty years ago, but Lord, *your name, your name* is in jeopardy. Unless you defend your own name I will surely let you down as I stand before all these people tomorrow morning with a sealed mouth, with nothing to say. You simply must defend your own name."

I went soundly to sleep. About 2:30 in the morning, I woke up fully alive. My heart was racing. My flesh was tingling. As I lay there, I heard very clearly, "The Church is the refuge of sinners."

I said, "No, that's Mary," because I recalled the Litany of Loretto very well.

I heard, "The Church is the comforter of the afflicted."

I said, "No, that's Mary."

Then, I heard, "The Church is Mary still on earth. The Church is always giving birth!"

I jumped out of bed, grabbed pencil and paper, and the Lord gave me an entire poem extolling the similarities between Mary and the Church. Here it is.

The Church

Ever virgin Bride of Christ,
Ever pregnant, housing life,
Ever youthful, ever new,
Ancient mother, full of grace!

Steeped in weakness, clothed in power
Bringing forth eternal Son,
The Church becomes Refuge of Sinners,
Comforter of the afflicted one!

Haven of the poor, the wretched,
Still attractive to the rich,
In the thick of battle always,
She is wounded, yet victorious!

Like a ship that's full of cargo
Does she roll on heavy seas,
Yet to men of every nation,
She becomes a place of rest.

Ever calling to her children,
For she knows them, every one,
Ever striving, ever yearning,
To become God's perfect Son!

Lighthouse on the distant shore,
Giving hope on stormy seas,
Sign of the Eternal Godhead,
Beckoning to all who wander far.

Repository of untold treasures,
Kings still seek to homage bring,
Yet the Church is poor and lowly,
Hidden stable of the King!

Geared for battle, on she presses,
Soaked with blood of Jesus Christ,
Still the ancient House of Israel,
Beloved of God, Beloved of Men.

Wounded, scoffed at and derided,
Still she bruises Satan's heel
And to those who know the story,
She reigns NOW in victory!

Ever crucified in Jesus,
Sometimes she seems dead to men.
Yet, Morning Star, she rises early
To give light and hope again!

The Church is Mary still on earth,
Always, ever, giving birth.
Courting sinners to restore them
To the Kingdom of the Son!

The Church is risen too in Jesus,
Still she struggles here on earth,

The Church is triumphant in glory,
The Church fills Mary's place on earth!

Moon reflecting Christ the Sun
Receiving life to pass it on,
The Church is meant to live forever,
The Church of Christ can never die!

The Church is Sign, the Church is Symbol,
The Church is Sacrament and Mystery,
The Church for sinners, House of Refuge,
For the righteous, House of Gold!

The Church, O Mystery yet unfathomed,
Will some great day be revealed:
Sons of God and Sons of Men!
Then we will all shout for glory,
Men and God forever ONE!

And Mary will be there among them,
Eternal Daughter of Eternal God,
Eternal Bride of Eternal Prince,
Eternal Mother of Eternal Word.

I gave my talk the next morning and said that the Church was born of the Spirit on Pentecost Sunday. The Church is the body of Christ, and it flowed from the wounded side of Christ in blood and water. On Pentecost Sunday, the Church became incarnate as the Holy Spirit fell upon them and they all became one in Christ. And then, I spoke of Mary being a symbol of the Church and then I read the poem.

Remember, this was an ecumenical gathering, with Protestants as well as Catholics. There were Evangelicals and Pentecostals, none of whom really understood the Church's devotion to Mary. I thought, "My God, they are going to lynch me!" But instead of that there was a hushed silence over the whole assembly as I gave the talk.

When I stopped talking, I had expected the bishop to have some words of correction, shall we say, but instead he came running across the stage, grabbed me in his arms and said, "Babsie, where did you get this? I have never heard such a dissertation on the Church."

I said, "Not me, sir, not me. It did not come from me."

Then seminarian Blackett (now Father Harcourt Blackett) said, "Auntie Babsie, everything that I have ever heard about our Lady and the Church you have expressed this morning."

Then Father Duffy, who was also there, came and said, "Babsie, dear, this is a most amazing revelation. It is so beautiful."

A Pentecostal representative, who also was to give a talk said, "Where have I been? Where have I been? Can I get a copy of this talk? I need to have a copy of this talk." In her talk she said, "If anyone here should doubt the presence of the Holy Spirit amongst us, listen to this. The same Scripture that Babsie ended her talk with is the Scripture I had to begin my talk on the Church." The entire assembly applauded. The Church present there experienced a moment of profound unity of spirit.

As a result of that, I realized the Lord was answering my prayers to help me know better his Mother and our Mother. I now realized that Mary would be relevant from age to age because she is Mother of Jesus and of the Body of Christ. She loves all her children throughout the ages. We have a perspective of the whole Church, as the body of Christ and as brothers and sisters of Jesus, being in Mary and Mary, as one of the body, being in the Church.

Our Holy Task: Bringing Christ to Others

The Church has been commissioned to do exactly what Mary did—to bring forth Christ every day, to give him away to the whole world and to bring forth sons and daughters of God every day in the sacrament of baptism. As Mary nourished Jesus, the Church is to nurture and nourish the whole family of God, to feed the people of God with the Bread of Life every day so they can grow strong in the Lord. As Mary comforted her Son when he was small and hurt himself, so the Church comforts her children and heals them through the sacrament of reconciliation.

As we yield to the Holy Spirit, we become other Marys, capable of bearing Jesus within our hearts and bringing him forth into the world to call all peoples into his Father's house.

The Church says, "Through Mary to Jesus." Mary is a stage each one of us must come through. We must be like Mary before we can fully be like Jesus, in Jesus, for Jesus and filled with Jesus. So, we see fulfilled the Scripture: "All of us, gazing with unveiled face on the glory of the Lord, are being transformed into the same image from glory to glory, as from the Lord who is the Spirit" (2 Cor 3:18). Mary is the first of the redeemed that has taken on this image and she has shown us how, and she is interested in our becoming like her to share in the redemptive work of Christ, to be, each one of us, as she is, a dispenser of the graces of the Church.

Mary wants us to let the Holy Spirit work through us so that we might be channels of grace as she was when she visited

Elizabeth. People should feel the presence of the Lord when we come near, that's how holy God wants us to be. That's how holy Mary was and how full of the Lord. We are to take as our life's commitment the revelation of Jesus to everyone we meet and to the whole world. That is the work of our lives.

So, in all this, I recalled the dream that had so puzzled me thirty years earlier—the dream of Mary weeping, consumed with sadness, as people passed her by on their way into the church. She knew her children were trying to get to Jesus but denying she could help them. She knew their hearts had not yet been sufficiently prepared to receive him fully.

Mary, Our Mother

Mary continues with her motherly care of us. She longs to see us walk in her footsteps and acquire her love for Jesus. She knows she can help us by her example and prayers. She does not want us to come to her and stay with her, but she wants to share with us her faith, her knowledge and wisdom, her very life and witness. Once we see Mary as the first disciple, as the first Christian, as one who is completely and totally consecrated to God, then we are better able to understand what it means to be a Christian and what it means to be the Church of Jesus Christ.

I began to pray a prayer from Mother Teresa: "Mary, Mother of Jesus, give me your heart, so beautiful, so pure, so immaculate, so full of love and humility that I may be able to receive Jesus in the Bread of Life, love him as you love him and serve him in the distressing disguise of the poorest of the poor." I actually sighed that prayer for a long time and eventually I addressed it to the Father:

"Father, recreate in me the miracle that you created in the heart of Mary when you made her holy and blameless by the action of your Holy Spirit so that she could receive Jesus, nurture him to full stature and give him away to the whole world, love him with her whole heart and serve him in the distressing disguise of the dissident apostles and the people who had brought him to his death."

As I prayed that prayer, I included the names of people who distressed me so I would have no grudges in my heart and so God would be able to recreate in me the miracle of the Immaculate Conception for the sake of Jesus. The Church can become holy and blameless if each of us has the heart of Mary to make a total and perfect response to the call of the Father for the sake of Jesus Christ.

Questions for Reflection

1. How has Mary been a part of your life? Have you ignored Mary? Have you stopped too short of Jesus and concentrated only on Mary?
2. Are you willing to surrender to the Holy Spirit so that you can become "pregnant" with Jesus to give him to the world? If so, pray for this grace with family and friends.
3. How can false humility stand in your way of total conversion and a vibrant life in the Spirit?

CHAPTER TWELVE

A Call to Action

IN THIS CLOSING CHAPTER, I want to share with you a prophetic vision that comes from different prophets in our Church. I also want to offer a few practical suggestions on how we can begin to respond to the call of John Paul II to enter into a "new springtime," into a new era of evangelization and perhaps, as some of us might say, a "new Pentecost."

St. Paul tells us (Rom 1:20-21), "Ever since the creation of the world, his *invisible attributes* of eternal power and divinity *have been able to be understood and perceived* in what he has made" (emphasis added). He says that people who have a perverse and irreligious spirit "have no excuse" because God makes himself known even through creation. These people "became vain in their reasoning, and their senseless minds were darkened."

Proof abounds in our world that many people do not experience the active presence of God in their lives. Life is not lived in the light of the Spirit. In fact, Pope John Paul II speaks of the culture of death that grips societies, leading them to infanticide, genocide and oppressions of all kinds. People seem to have lost their ability to discern what is real and what is fake. They believe the rhetoric of politicians rather than evaluate the service of politicians. They believe the fantasies of movies, and imitate false images of masculinity and femininity.

This penchant for fantasy makes it harder for people to come to grips with reality. People become accustomed to fakes and fakery, to imitations and artificiality. Fantasy invades religion and weakens faith with sentimental superficiality.

The attraction of fantasies and imitations is evidenced all around us, in our homes and marketplaces. So much passes for real that is only cheap imitation. If we are taken in by fantasy, we will not easily focus on our need to rekindle and refresh our life in the Spirit of the living and holy God. For to live in the Spirit is to call a lie a lie, and to speak, to defend, and to live the truth.

Plastic Prophets?

I returned from Israel once with a beautiful pin that I thought was mother of pearl. But when I had to repair it, it was plastic. I went to visit my daughter who said, "Mother, what a beautiful pin! Is it mother of pearl?" I started to reply, "When I bought it I thought so, but I discovered ..." and she interrupted me, "But you discovered it was mother of plastic!" We laughed loudly together.

Another time, my dear friends, Deacon Henry and Peggy Libersat, bought a bird of paradise with a beautiful bloom for their front yard in Florida. It was the longest-lasting bloom ever. One day, they commented on how long the bloom had lasted, walked over and touched it, and it fell over! The plant was real, but the bloom was fake!

There is so much confusion today about God, about what is right and what is wrong. We truly need the Church and all the Church gives us to help us know God, and to love and serve him. There are fake notions about God, religious fakes, people who claim to know God and serve him but instead make up their own "gospel" to please themselves and their followers.

There is a great need today for truth, for the real gospel of the Lord. In short, there is a great need for genuine prophecy. I want to look again, briefly, at the ministry of the prophet, as I mentioned I would do. The prophet calls people to task when they go astray. He speaks God's "now message" to his people. The prophet places modern times and troubles in the context of all Scripture and the teachings of the Church. God gives the prophetic gifts freely to the whole Church, and to some who have prophecy as a ministry.

Prophecy is real. When I hear a truly prophetic word, I stop what I am doing and I listen with all my heart. Bishop Fulton J. Sheen, in his last retreat to priests, spoke a prophetic word. He said that by the end of the twentieth century anyone who would witness to Christ must have become Christ. The Gospel will demand no less than that, for men are worn out with words—words that have brought forth no fruit—and with vain promises in all aspects of our lives.

So the disciple of Christ must allow the Holy Spirit to so transform him, that his whole life will be the witness to the gospel. And we are already beginning to see that happen. People are not listening to words. But they are deeply moved and inspired by the life of Mother Teresa. They may disagree with some of the prophetic words of Pope John Paul, but they love him for who he is and respect his total surrender to God and his concern for the good of all peoples. They marvel at his dedication and commitment to the gospel and to justice and peace.

So, as we approach the end of this century, and spring with

hope and joy into the next, we realize we must become so like Christ that we become martyrs for him. We so love him and commit ourselves to him that we lay down our lives to take up his own. We pray to be willing to lay down our lives, even to actual bloody martyrdom, if that is his will and if that is what it takes to convince people of his lordship and his saving grace. This is a time when we should allow the Holy Spirit to prepare us. We must become so docile to the Spirit that we will be able to hear his slightest whisper and be willing to obey as soon as we recognize his voice. We must hear his voice, even as Elijah the prophet heard his voice:

> *Then the Lord said, "Go outside and stand on the mountain before the Lord; the Lord will be passing by." A strong and heavy wind was rending the mountains and crushing rocks before the Lord—but the Lord was not in the wind. After the wind there was an earthquake—but the Lord was not in the earthquake.*
>
> *After the earthquake there was fire—but the Lord was not in the fire. After the fire there was a tiny whispering sound.*
>
> *When he heard this, Elijah hid his face in his cloak and went and stood at the entrance of the cave.*
>
> 1 KINGS 19:11-13

Called to Be Like Christ

As we are challenged day to day, we realize that the Lord brings us to the places where we have a rare confrontation with ourselves. We come to know, without a doubt, our weaknesses and our failures. We recognize our insufficiencies and our need to hold on to Jesus.

I believe that this confrontation with ourselves, as individuals and as the Church, will continue and increase in intensity over the next few years. It will continue until we who are sensitive to the Spirit realize that the Spirit will never be satisfied until the first word on our lips is the name of Jesus.

Our need will never be met by other people, by the acquisition of material things or higher degrees or greater honors on earth. Our need will only be met by total reliance on the power of the Holy Spirit and on Jesus Christ as Lord and Savior.

I am reminded of Jesus' admonition to the crowds—and to us today (Lk 12:54-56): "When you see [a] cloud rising in the west you say immediately that it is going to rain—and so it does; and when the wind is blowing from the south you say that it is going to be hot—and so it is. You hypocrites! You know how to interpret the appearance of the earth and the sky; why do you not know how to interpret the present time?"

Signs of the Times

Jesus truly expects us to be able to tell what time it is in God's calendar. He went into great detail in the Gospels of Luke and Matthew to describe what the time of the coming of the kingdom would be like. He said there would be great tribulation, natural catastrophes, wars and rumors of wars; that hardness of heart would overtake us, and children and parents would turn from one another. As we look around us, we see that these things are evident everywhere.

The more sensitive we are to the Holy Spirit—and the more we allow the Spirit to renew our minds so we can see with the eyes of Jesus, hear with his ears and discern with his heart—it seems that "all creation is groaning in labor pains even until now." Creation itself seems to be groaning in labor pains for deliverance from the futility placed upon it when man fell in the Garden of Eden (Rom 8:20-27).

We remember that whenever God was birthing a new era, when he was bringing into the world a person who would play a marked part in the history of the world, we saw the slaughter of innocents. When Moses was coming into the world to deliver the Israelites, there was a slaughter of innocents. All the male children of Israel, by Egyptian decrees, were to be killed at birth. Moses escaped by God's will carried out by his mother, a midwife, his sister Miriam, and the pagan daughter of Pharaoh who raised him as her own.

Again when Jesus came into the world, Herod, afraid for his own kingdom, commanded that all Hebrew males under two years of age be slaughtered. But Joseph, forewarned in a dream and docile to the Holy Spirit, took Mary and the Child and fled. Many babies were slaughtered. But Jesus lived on, according to the Father's will, to minister, to preach, teach, and heal and finally to die on the cross so we might be saved.

When Moses was saved, the Israelites passed over from slavery into freedom. When Jesus was saved, Israel passed over from Judaism to Christianity. It seems that prophetically the slaughter of innocents is a precursor to a passover.

Now we have the present day slaughter of innocents through abortion and infanticide. We have the abuse of little children by the pornography industry and uncaring parents, and by sick people who sexually assault them. In some countries, homeless children living in the streets are shot as though they are rodents. *If there is a relationship between the abuse of the innocents and God's intervention in a special way in the world, then God may well be getting ready to reveal to the world his perfected sons and daughters.* He may well be ready to hold up before the world those sons and daughters who have been restored into his image and likeness.

The Spirit and the Church to Come

Hence, Pope John Paul II sees a Church that will be experiencing a new springtime, a Church filled with the glory of God. The prophetic vision, among those who are exercising these gifts over the last thirty years, seems to be that we are looking forward to a Church in which every member will be a firstborn son. A Church so infused by the power of the Holy Spirit that anyone entering will immediately be healed. A Church in which any sinner entering the assembly of faithful will have a head-on confrontation with Jesus, and experience deep repentance.

We see this new Church as exuberant and alive, a Church that has never been seen before, a Church in which we will be truly devoted to "the teaching of the apostles and to the communal life, to the breaking of the bread and to the prayers" (Acts 2:42).

This is the prophetic vision for the new millennium, a Church that is full of the presence and the power of God. When this comes to pass, we will embrace, with new fervor, commitment and joy, Jesus, the Lord of the Church. The Church will once again give the Word to the world instead of receiving the word of the world.

I am reminded of a prophecy brought by St. John Bosco in the nineteenth century. He said, back in 1862, that there would be an ecumenical council in the next (twentieth) century after which there would be chaos in the Church. Tranquillity, he said, would not return until the pope succeeds in anchoring the boat of Peter between the twin pillars of eucharistic adoration and true devotion to our Lady, Mary. *This will come about, he said, one year before the end of the twentieth century.*

And, for the discerning eyes, there are already signs that this is beginning to happen. Eucharistic devotion and devotion to Mary are increasing in the Church due in no small part to the ministry of Pope John Paul II. So, it seems we are in an important time in the history of the Church and the world.

I hope I have convinced you of the importance of the prophetic word in our own generation and how it helps us to hear what God wants of us.

So, How Do We Respond to the Spirit?

To respond to the call of the Holy Spirit through our Holy Father, we must develop a true sensitivity for the Church, for the body of Christ. We must, through prayer and reflection, become a "nerve ending" that can feel what Jesus feels.

In Trinidad, we had a deeply moving experience. A prophetic word said we must not spurn the broken body of Christ, his divided Church. But we had to weep over it. *"Take the broken body into your arms, press it into your bosom. Weep over it and cleanse it with your tears. Pray for her, for I will restore her. She is my bride and I love her and I will restore her."*

That prophetic word stirred many of us to pray for the Church and in fact, as a result of that prophetic word, people in Trinidad continue to pray for the Church and its leaders with deep fervor.

Another instance occurred at a national ecumenical conference in Kansas City in 1977 when Ralph Martin had a prophetic word that the body of Christ should weep and repent over the divisions in the Church. The entire assembly was moved to weep with deep sorrow over the disunity among Christians.

We must all develop that kind of sensitivity to the Church. We must suffer and rejoice with the Church for we are all part of that one body. Participation in the sacrifice of the Mass, a deep prayer life and helping those in need will surely help Catholics develop that kind of sensitivity.

Be Aware of the Power of Prayer

Most of us have heard of or prayed the prayer to St. Michael the Archangel. (For your convenience, that prayer is provided, among others, in the appendix at the end of this book.) Pope Leo XIII was pope from 1878 to 1903. One morning after Mass, as he was purifying the sacred vessels, he had a vision. He heard Satan challenging Jesus. Satan said that he could destroy the Church if given enought time. Christ gave him leave to try. After the vision was over, Leo XIII sat down and wrote the prayer of St. Michael that was used at the end of every Mass throughout the world until Vatican Council II.

Even with this prayer, we saw World War II and the ravages visited upon man by Nazi Germany. The Holocaust stands as one of the most despicable and terrifying events in the history of the world. We know the free world finally won. Even communism was defeated. But, since the Church has stopped praying that prayer as a body, it seems we have seen more of the ravages of evil, the continuous wars, the rise in crime and terrorism, abuse of women and children and of the aged, the inhumanity of one man to another.

Pope John Paul II, in his document on the third millennium, records all the atrocities of two world wars and observes "All these events demonstrate most vividly that the world needs purification; it needs to be converted" (par 18).

And yet he looks toward the third millennium with a great

deal of hope, and urges us to do the same. We need to refresh our lives in the Spirit. A life of sincere trust in God and prayer will give us the kind of hope we need to convince the world that Jesus is alive and able to help us all.

A Call to Forgiveness and Reconciliation

The Holy Father calls for this Jubilee, this Holy Year 2000, in the Old Testament understanding of jubilee. He reminds us that in Old Testament times, a jubilee year was a year of forgiveness. Slaves were freed. People who had lost property had their property returned. For those who were in deep debt, the debt was written off. It was a whole year of forgiveness and a year of rejoicing when the nation, the people of God, basked in the favor of God.

In his prophetic vision, Pope John Paul promises us that the year 2000 will be a year when we will experience the favor of God very deeply. In the midst of this, there will be a new springtime for the Church as we experience forgiveness of sin. He exhorts us to prepare for this great jubilee by repentance, mortification and examination of conscience. God's desire is that every man who comes to know his sins will be moved to repent and make peace with God. It is God's mercy that will lead us to see our sinful condition.

Pope John Paul II calls us to examine our own consciences, to let the light of the Holy Spirit flood our lives and the deepest recesses of our souls and memories so we might come to know our need for forgiveness. As we receive the forgiveness of God, we will be able to accept it and as we are forgiven by God, we can forgive one another and make peace with one another. We can become docile to the Holy Spirit so the Lord might be able to effect among us the coming of this new springtime in which the Church will be renewed and restored by the power of the Holy Spirit.

A Call to Evangelization

In this prophetic vision, and in response to the call of Pope John Paul, there will be a great era of evangelization in the years ahead. Each person who knows Jesus will be able to share his faith by the grace and power of the Holy Spirit. It is the Spirit who is the true evangelizer. He it is who prepares us to receive the word, and helps us share the word effectively to bring others to Christ.

Deacon Henry, my coauthor and editor of a leading Catholic newspaper in North America, has read that throughout the world a growing number of Catholics are responding to the Holy Spirit. Some have already begun to fast, pray and repent. Lay people are taking leadership in parishes to increase love for Jesus through sharing Scripture. Some parishes are rediscovering the power of small prayer groups. Rosary groups are increasing in number. Lay people, under the leadership of their priests, are seeking ways in which to help Catholics become more comfortable and effective in sharing their Catholic faith. Dioceses are expanding communications ministries to include more outreach by radio. In Florida, for example, Catholic newspapers are working with Catholic radio ministries to bring more attention to the Holy Father's call to Jubilee 2000.

Catholics who are shy about sharing their faith can do two things: First, they can ask their priests and parish catechists to help them become more knowledgeable about their faith and more comfortable in sharing it. Secondly, they can pray fervently to the Holy Spirit for complete conversion and total transformation into the image, heart and mind of Jesus.

Pope John Paul II hopes that by the end of this century, at least half the world will truly have heard the Gospel of Jesus Christ. He calls every one of us to be ready for this period of evangelization. When we celebrate the great birthday party on December 25, 2000, not one of us should appear at this party without a gift of at least one soul in our hands.

The cry of Jesus remains, "I thirst!" Just as he cried out from the cross, he cries out today, "I thirst!" And his thirst will only be assuaged by the winning of souls. He still thirsts for souls.

Remember the Power of the Saints

The communion of saints! It is not only a doctrine, but a wonderful reality. The saints led prophetic lives. By reflecting on their lives and praying with them, we can learn more about being good Catholics. If we do not believe in the communion of the saints, we impoverish our spirits. I know from experience how helpful it is to be on speaking terms with those who have gone before us and who now, as we know through the faith and authority of the Church, are with Christ and can pray with us and for us.

The Letter to the Hebrews becomes very illuminating in this context: "You have approached Mount Zion and the city of the living God, the heavenly Jerusalem and countless angels in festal gathering, and the assembly of the firstborn enrolled in heaven " (Heb 12:22-23).

Let me give you a little insight into my own experience with one of the Lord's great saints. From my earliest years, I had a great devotion to St. Anthony. Many know him as the saint who helps us find lost things. St. Anthony was born in Portugal in 1195 and died in 1231. He was a great priest and preacher. He was canonized a saint a mere year after his death at thirty-six years of age. He is often depicted holding the Child Jesus in his arms.

In 1974, I had a special encounter with him. A granddaughter's illness threatened to keep me away from the celebration of his feast day in New York. So I chided St. Anthony: "Now, I am sure you are displeased with me. Why would you not help me as I pray for my granddaughter to get well so I would be able to attend your feast?"

As I prayed, I had a significant spiritual experience. Space does not permit a lengthy version of this story, but Our Lady appeared with the Child and also St. Anthony. In the last part of the vision, St. Anthony had his back to me and I could see the Child over his shoulder. He pushed the Child over his shoulder, as far as his extended arms could go, and he said to me, "I have brought you to Jesus. Stop bugging me! You and I have now joined the communion of saints. Get on your knees and do for others what I have done for you!"

I didn't want to believe I had to assume this responsibility. I didn't know why I felt so reticent. But I said, "Jesus, I will do it. Holy Spirit, help me and I will do it."

I related that experience to a priest. He jumped up from his chair and said, "Ah! Babsie, I am so happy you told me this story! That's precisely the work of the saints, to bring us to Jesus and once they bring us to Jesus we must participate in their work of bringing others to Jesus." I thought, "How true! Then I won't let Anthony down. I won't let the Spirit down. I won't let Jesus down." This threw me full swing into the work of evangelization in which I have been involved for nearly twenty-five years. How great is God! How wonderful his ways!

That is only one example of how the communion of saints is an important reality in our lives.

By Testimony and Experience

This is what Pope John Paul II is asking of us, that we become so inspired by God's love for us and the joy of forgiveness that we make Jesus known at every opportunity and in all situations. There is no vacation from our vocation to fulfill the mission of Jesus.

As we prepare for Jubilee 2000, let us pray that we might recognize the Word of God. We need to pray with all our hearts for the gift of humility so that each of us might become like Mary, completely docile to the Holy Spirit. We must be so humble and docile that the Lord can work in us and through us this transformation of hearts, so each of our hearts may become like the heart of Mary, and the Church may pass through the image of Mary into the image of Christ.

We must be so radically changed that our very lives are prophetic. Then the prophecy of Bishop Sheen will be fulfilled. We will be so transformed we will hold hands and gaze together on the face of the Son and be changed from glory to glory into his image. We will continuously sigh from the depths of our beings, "Come, Holy Spirit! Come, Lord Jesus!" And we will see the kingdom of God established on earth. The prayer of Jesus Christ, that we be one as he and the Father are one, will at last be realized. And the prayer we have prayed for so many centuries will finally be answered:

THY KINGDOM COME!
THY WILL BE DONE!

To achieve that end by and through the grace of God, to rekindle and refresh our life in the Spirit, let us pray from deep within our hearts:

"Lord, yours is the harvest and yours is the vineyard. You assign the task and you pay a wage that is just. Help me to be faithful in all my responsibilities today and never let me be separated from you. Amen.

Amen and amen!

APPENDIX

Basic Prayers for Catholics

The Lord's Prayer

Our Father, who art in heaven, hallowed be thy name. Thy kingdom come. Thy will be done on earth as it is in heaven. Give us this day our daily bread, and forgive us our trespasses as we forgive those who trespass against us, and lead us not into temptation, but deliver us from evil.

Hail Mary

Hail Mary, full of grace. The Lord is with thee. Blessed art thou among women, and blessed is the fruit of thy womb, Jesus. Holy Mary, Mother of God, pray for us sinners now and at the hour of our death. Amen.

The Doxology (Glory Be...)

Glory be to the Father and to the Son and to the Holy Spirit, as it was in the beginning, is now and ever shall be, world without end. Amen.

Prayer to the Holy Spirit

Come Holy Spirit, fill the hearts of thy faithful and enkindle in us the fire of thy divine love. Send forth thy Spirit and they shall be created, and thou shalt renew the face of the earth.

The Apostles' Creed

I believe in God, the Father Almighty, Creator of heaven and earth, and in Jesus Christ his only Son, our Lord, who was conceived by the Holy Spirit, born of the Virgin Mary, suffered under Pontius Pilate, was crucified, died and was buried. He descended into hell; the third day he arose again from the dead. He ascended into heaven, and is seated at the right hand of the Father. From thence he shall come to judge the living and the dead. I believe in the Holy Spirit, the Holy Catholic Church, the communion of saints, the forgiveness of sins, the resurrection of the body and life everlasting. Amen.

The Act of Contrition

O my God, I am heartily sorry for having offended thee. And I detest all my sins because of your just punishments, but most of all because they offend thee, my God, who art all good and deserving of all my love. I firmly resolve, with the help of thy grace, to sin no more and to avoid the near occasions of sin.

The Hail Holy Queen

Hail Holy Queen, Mother of mercy, our life, our sweetness and our hope. To thee do we cry, poor banished children of Eve. To thee do we send up our sighs, mourning and weeping in this vale of tears. Turn then, most gracious advocate, thine eyes of mercy toward us, and after this our exile, show unto us the blessed fruit of thy womb, Jesus. O clement, O loving, O sweet Virgin Mary.

Pray for us, O holy Mother of God, that we may be worthy of the promises of Christ.

Prayer for the Church

Let us pray. O God, our refuge and our strength! Look down with mercy on thy people who cry out to thee. And through the intercession of the glorious and immaculate Virgin Mary, Mother of God, and of her spouse, Blessed Joseph, of thy holy apostles, Peter and Paul, and all the saints, mercifully and graciously hear the prayers we pour forth for the conversion of sinners and for the freedom and exaltation of Holy Mother Church throughout the world. Amen.

Prayer to St. Michael

St. Michael the Archangel, defend us in battle. Be our protection against the wickedness and snares of the devil. May God rebuke him, we humbly pray, and do thou, O Prince of the Heavenly Hosts, cast into hell Satan and all the other evil spirits who roam through the world seeking the ruin of souls. Amen.

The Mysteries of the Rosary

Joyful mysteries: Annunciation, Visitation, Birth of our Savior, Presentation in the Temple, Finding Jesus in the Temple.

Sorrowful mysteries: Agony in the Garden, the Scourging of Jesus, the Crowning with Thorns, the Carrying of the Cross, the Crucifixion.

The Glorious Mysteries: The Resurrection, the Ascension, the Coming of the Holy Spirit, the Assumption of Mary into Heaven, the Coronation of Mary as Queen of Heaven.

spiritual
renewal

5543

DATE DUE			